It Happened In Hollywood

Remarkable Events That Shaped History

Gerald A. Schiller

D1417479

Guilford, Connecticut

Copyright © 2010 by Morris Book Publishing, LLC

Project editor: David Legere
Map: M.A. Dubé © Morris Book Publishing, LLC

Library of Congress Cataloging-in-Publication Data
Schiller, Gerald A. (Gerald Alan), 1936-
  It happened in Hollywood : remarkable events that shaped history / Gerald A. Schiller.
      p. cm.
  Includes bibliographical references and index.
  ISBN 978-0-7627-5449-6
  1. Motion picture industry—California—Los Angeles—History—20th century—
Anecdotes. 2. Motion picture actors and actresses—California—Los Angeles—
Biography—Anecdotes. 3. Motion picture producers and directors—California—Los
Angeles—Biography—Anecdotes. 4. Hollywood (Los Angeles, Calif.)—History—
20th century—Anecdotes. 5. Hollywood (Los Angeles, Calif.)—Biography—
Anecdotes. 6. Los Angeles (Calif.)—History—20th century—Anecdotes. 7. Los
Angeles (Calif.)—Biography—Anecdotes. I. Title.
  PN1993.5.U65S33 2010
  384'.80979494—dc22

                                                                          2009036926

Printed in the United States of America

10 9 8 7 6 5 4 3 2 1

To Esther

HOLLYWOOD

GLENDALE

EAST
LOS ANGELES

2

134

5

MACK SENNETT
STUDIES

SILVER
LAKE

110

101

DOWNTOWN
LOS ANGELES

WESTLAKE

SITE OF
BABYLON SET
FOR *Intolerance*

HOLLYWOOD

LASKY
STUDIO

CHARLIE CHAPLIN
STUDIOS

KOREATOWN

110

CURRENT
DISNEY
STUDIOS

BURBANK

HOLLYWOOD
SIGN

170

MAGIC CASTLE

CENTRAL
LOS ANGELES

UNIVERSAL
STUDIOS

HOLLYWOOD
ROOSEVELT HOTEL

WEST
HOLLYWOOD

2

CURRENT
WARNER BROS.
STUDIOS

HOLLYWOOD
HILLS

SANTA MONICA

MOUNTAINS

VAN NUYS

BEVERLY
HILLS

BEVERLY GLEN

TWENTIETH
CENTURY
FOX STUDIOS

405

MGM
STUDIOS

CULVER CITY

101

BEL-AIR

CENTURY
CITY

405

SANTA MONICA

BRENTWOOD

2

1

PACIFIC PALISADES

1

*Pacific
Ocean*

N

0   1.5   3 KILOMETERS
0   1.5   3 MILES

CONTENTS

CONTENTS

INTRODUCTION

Although you can easily find Hollywood on a Los Angeles map, it's a community that, in many ways, defies geography.

The film studios are scattered all over: Twentieth Century Fox in West Los Angeles, Metro-Goldwyn-Mayer in Culver City, Walt Disney Studios in Burbank, and many smaller film-production companies in Santa Monica and the San Fernando Valley. The headquarters of the Academy of Motion Picture Arts and Sciences (the organization that gives out the Oscars each year) is located in Beverly Hills. For years announcer Ed McMahon introduced Johnny Carson's late-night show by intoning, "From Hollywood, it's *The Tonight Show* with Johnny Carson!" yet the program was taped at the NBC-TV studios in Burbank. We associate these centers of production, however, as being part of "Hollywood."

More than just a place, then, Hollywood has become a term that symbolizes film and television production, and although more than half of the films we might see at our local multiplex have probably been made in New York, Canada, Europe, or Asia, we still call many of them "Hollywood" movies.

Many of the stories that follow did not happen precisely in that suburb of Los Angeles that the map designates as Hollywood, yet in many ways they are still very much Hollywood stories. This is because all of them are closely related to the movie business. It was a business where, almost a hundred years ago, a hearty band of entrepreneurs made the trek west from New York and New Jersey. In Southern California they discovered, to their amazement, a climate in which they could film outdoors almost any day of the year; fabulous locations with mountains, deserts, and an ocean; and a ready supply of people to fill all kinds of jobs. There was also another advantage: California was a long distance from New York. At the time there were several legal struggles going on over equipment patents and other business disagreements, and Southern California provided easy access for slipping across the border into Mexico to escape subpoenas!

Hollywood stories, however, are not always those of excitement, wonder, and discovery. You'll also find a healthy share of scandal, disaster, and tragedy. And since Hollywood has always provided excellent fodder for news stories, the press has, perhaps too eagerly, picked on the film capital for juicy tales they felt would interest—and titillate—their audiences.

What follows are stories of those who came to Hollywood and thrived, like the filmmaker D. W. Griffith, whose epic films laid the groundwork for an entire industry, yet who, in many ways, was years ahead of his time. There are those like Mack Sennett, who learned how to make moving pictures that moved—at breakneck pace—where laughs piled up in rapid-fire succession. There's Charlie Chaplin, who grew up in poverty but whose name, because of Hollywood, would eventually be known all over the world, and Walt Disney, a man whose name would live on long after his death as a symbol of family entertainment.

You'll find tales of films that succeeded and films that flopped, and the story of the film that changed everything because it talked. Here are the people and the events that were famous and those that were infamous, and, of course, the stories of the Hollywood tragedies: the drugs, the deaths, the accidents.

So, good and bad, successful and tragic, happy and sad—all of these are Hollywood stories, each of them a compelling tale of an exotic and magical place that, like the movies themselves, almost always manages to fascinate, thrill, and captivate an audience.

A SLEEPY LITTLE TOWN
GETS INVADED

1910

The thin man with a delicate French accent was intrigued. He needed a place to set up his studio—a quiet place where he could paint the flowers he loved so much. But in New York City flowers were just too costly, too hard to find in the winter, and definitely lacking in variety.

A woman, a Mrs. Wilcox, had approached him and suggested he visit Southern California, where it just so happened her late husband, Harvey Henderson Wilcox, had developed some property. She told the artist that the flowers there were magnificent, there was an infinite variety of blooms, and, best of all, the sun shined almost 350 days each year. When the artist, whose name was Paul Delongpre, asked her what the area was called, she explained that while it was originally referred to as Wilcox Ranch, she preferred the more romantic name, Hollywood.

Delongpre was definitely interested. He made the trip and liked what he saw. So in 1902, in exchange for three of his floral paintings, he acquired a lot and ultimately had a large mansion built on it. The manse was surrounded by a luxuriant garden, and it quickly became a tourist attraction.

The town Delongpre had settled in had evolved from a single adobe hut in 1853 to a thriving agricultural community. Several theories on the origin of the name "Hollywood" have been suggested. One involves the bright red berries that appear on the native toyon bushes that proliferate in the area, which some called the "California holly." Another theory suggests that early settlers brought real holly when they came west. Probably the real story is that the name was coined by H. J. Whitley and his wife, Gigi, who in 1886 were on their honeymoon in the area and just came up with the name.

In 1900 the community had a post office, newspaper, hotel, and two markets, and its population numbered about five hundred. A streetcar ran along the main street, Prospect Avenue (later known as Hollywood Boulevard), eastward for ten miles to downtown Los Angeles, a trip that could take as much as two hours. Incorporated in 1903, the town fathers passed ordinances that prohibited the sale of alcohol (except by pharmacists) and forbade the driving of cattle through the town's streets—if the herd contained more than two hundred animals.

By 1910 the little town of Hollywood continued to add new residents, but there were problems. One of them was water, so the town voted to become part of nearby Los Angeles to have access to the water supply from the Owens River. It has been part of Los Angeles ever since, though a few attempts have been made over the years to make it a separate city.

In 1910 there were only a few paved roads, some automobiles, and one policeman who directed the minimal traffic from his spot at Hollywood Boulevard and Vine Street. The town, however, was not just being visited by health seekers and the curious—occasionally filmmakers, looking for a place to work during the cold eastern winters, showed up.

At the turn of the century, movies were a mere curiosity. They might last for a few seconds, as a person cranked a handle and peered through a hole in a box at a train chugging into a station or a dancer doing a few steps. But by 1910 a lot had changed. Now they were being projected onto screens: travelogues of faraway places, comedies with raucous humor, serious stories of love and tragedy. And there was a ready and eager audience paying a nickel or a dime each week to see the latest of these new attractions.

Though Hollywood's town fathers banned the sale of alcohol, they did not consider banning movie people, assuming that they, like traveling actors, would not stay long. And for several years, that is exactly what happened. With film production centered in New York and New Jersey, Southern California was just a temporary location to work on movies until the eastern weather became more temperate.

One of the filmmakers who made the trek west with a company of actors and technicians was a man by the name of David Wark Griffith. He had started his movie career as an actor, but soon was given a chance to direct some of the ten-minute dramas that Biograph, the company that employed him, was noted for. By 1910 he had a well-established reputation and had made dozens of short films. He was respected enough to convince his bosses that Southern California was the best place for him to make his films in the winter.

When Griffith's actors and crew arrived, they discovered that many of the accommodations were primitive: A large lot surrounded by a fence was their first studio, a few ramshackle buildings served as dressing rooms, and a wooden platform that was open to the air was to be used for interior scenes. But Griffith was intrigued by the lore of the West and decided to utilize California as a background for stories that were inherently local—films about miners, oppressed

Indians, and life in Mexico—using locations like the mountains and the California missions.

When Griffith needed a garden for a film called *Love Among the Roses,* he approached painter Paul Delongpre and offered him $50 a day to use his luxuriant grounds. The artist offered the filmmaker a better deal: For just $300, he could buy an entire lot on nearby Hollywood Boulevard. But Griffith was not interested. He couldn't conceive of owning property in Hollywood; to him, it was just a temporary place to visit and make some movies.

That first year in California (1910), Griffith and his company made about twenty films, including one called *In Old California,* which has the official distinction of being the very first movie actually made in Hollywood. He then returned to the East Coast, and came back each winter for the next three years.

In the meantime, other movie companies were catching on to the advantages of shooting in California. And it was not just the weather and the locations: There was a ready supply of cheap labor—with no unions anywhere in sight. Yet even as the area grew, it still had a small-town feel to it. Some ultraconservative residents refused to associate with the movie folks, even keeping their children away from the "theatrical types." Many others, however, welcomed them, rented rooms to them, and looked forward to picking up work with the film companies.

As one veteran performer described those days: Once the word was out, every morning eager local residents would rush to the gates of the new studios to look for work. If one company had nothing, the crowd would rush to another lot in the hope that they were hiring that day. Saturdays and Sundays and holidays didn't matter, if there was work. As a bonus, since the average one-reel (ten-minute) production was completed in about a week, it was not uncommon for the whole neighborhood to be called in to watch a screening of a newly produced movie.

So it was that an invasion had begun—and Hollywood would never be the same again.

MACK BUILDS A FUN FACTORY

1912

They were wild. They were fast. They were filled with breakneck activity. They were hilariously funny. Most of all, the public loved them.

They were the short films produced by Keystone Studios, which was created by a man named Mack Sennett. It was a studio that launched the careers of many individuals who went on to become popular and successful silent film comedians.

On January 17, 1880, in Richmond, Quebec, Canada, Michael Sinnott was born, the son of immigrant farmers. In 1897 the family moved to the United States, where Michael's mother ran a boardinghouse. Bitten early by the acting bug, nineteen-year-old Michael went from his home in Connecticut to New York City and picked up some bit parts in plays, as well as doing some singing in choruses with his booming bass voice.

By 1908 Michael had changed his name to Mack Sennett and decided to try his hand in the movies. The Biograph studio was in New York, so he visited the facility and was soon doing parts in the short silent films they ground out on an almost daily basis. Sennett quickly learned a lot about movies—especially when he met David Wark Griffith, a very creative Biograph employee who had advanced from acting to directing. Soon Sennett was earning additional money by submitting stories for the films, and shortly thereafter he was directing and acting in a series of comedy films at a salary of $50 per week.

In 1912 the thirty-two-year-old Sennett, now working for Adam Kessel and Charles Bauman's New York Motion Picture Company, was put in charge of a company called Keystone and sent to California. His job was to produce a steady supply of comedy films to fill the rapidly growing public demand. It was a responsibility he was to fulfill with much more than ordinary skill and artistry, as he was about to create a whole new art: the slapstick silent comedy. And Mack Sennett would be its master.

In Edendale, a suburb just east of Hollywood, Sennett assembled a group of skilled performers and began to produce some of the most hilarious films ever made in all of movie history. The themes of the Keystone comedies covered the whole range of human behavior, generally carried to some ridiculous extent. They made fun of the police, the clergy, the wealthy, and anyone who showed some pretentious behavior. Marital mix-ups were often their subject, as was almost any silly situation they could come up with.

Perhaps Sennett's most lasting creation was that of the Keystone Kops. They became so popular that the term "Keystone Kops" is still used today to refer to any bumbling, ridiculous group that is unable to accomplish even the simplest task. The Kops first showed up in the 1913 film *The Bangville Police*. Soon they were appearing regularly, being flung off their autos, almost run over by trains, dragged behind vehicles, and suffering every kind of mishap but never getting hurt.

In the Keystone comedies, gags had to follow quickly, building to bigger and bigger laughs. The worst offense at a Sennett film was silence in the theater, so his performers (and directors) quickly learned how to pace the funny situations.

One of Keystone's most popular gags was the pie thrown in the face. The first film to utilize this device was probably *A Noise from the Deep* in 1913. Comedienne Mabel Normand threw it, and Roscoe "Fatty" Arbuckle got hit. Soon pie-throwing became a frequent bit in Keystone comedies. Interestingly, the pies used were rarely edible ones. They were either filled with paste or with blackberries covered with whipped cream. Custard wouldn't hold together well enough as the pies sailed from several feet away before meeting their target in an unsuspecting victim's face.

Among the many actors who started with Sennett were Charlie Chaplin, Mabel Normand, "Fatty" Arbuckle, Gloria Swanson—and, later, Bing Crosby and W. C. Fields. Unfortunately, many did not stay long because Sennett was notoriously cheap and often, as in the case of Chaplin, refused to pay the salaries the performers demanded, even though their films were highly successful and, as with Chaplin, theater owners clamored for more of them.

By 1914 Sennett's Keystone Studios were producing some of the most popular short films in the country, and business was booming. The studio was expanded to turn out more product, and soon there were three stages in constant operation and eight directors working steadily.

Sennett also felt that it was time to expand the length of his films and venture into a production that was an hour or more long. He knew that his old friend from the Biograph days, David Wark Griffith, was at work on a long, epic film (which would ultimately be called *The Birth of a Nation*), and he wanted to do the same with a comedy. He was eventually able to sell Kessel and Bauman on the idea—although he had to put his one-third interest in the company on the line—and got them to put up the

$50,000 needed for the project. He was also able to get popular stage actress Marie Dressler to act in the film at a salary of $2,500 per week, and, along with Charlie Chaplin (who was already on salary), they produced *Tillie's Punctured Romance.* The film turned out to be highly profitable.

It would, however, be Chaplin's virtual swan song for Keystone. Although he had two more short films to finish for the studio, he and Sennett could not agree on a new salary. The comedian wanted $750 per week with built-in increases, but this was more than the studio was willing to offer, so Charlie parted company with Keystone. Just a short time later, when Chaplin signed with the Essanay Company, Sennet was astonished to discover that the salary they agreed to pay him was an amazing $1,250 weekly.

Another of Keystone's popular performers was comedienne Mabel Normand. She and Sennett had had an "on again, off again" romantic relationship over the years, but for various reasons it never culminated in marriage. Mabel had been quite ill with pneumonia, but returned to Keystone in 1916 to do a six-reel (one-hour) film called *Mickey.* When Kessel and Bauman saw it, however, they were appalled. It lacked all the knockabout elements of a Keystone film. Instead, it was a light, romantic comedy with Mabel as the daughter of a prospector who goes to New York.

Ironically, even though the film was initially shelved, it was released two years later in 1918 and proved a delight to audiences. It played for four years, grossing over $18 million. With her own company, Normand made several films after *Mickey,* before dying of tuberculosis in 1930 at the age of thirty-seven.

By 1917 Sennett himself left Keystone following a series of disputes with the owners. He would go on to produce films under the name Mack Sennett Comedies, making both features and short films with considerable success. He also produced some sound films in the

1930s, but in November 1933 his production company was forced into bankruptcy, a victim of the Great Depression.

During his career Mack Sennett and his Keystone Studios produced more than a thousand silent comedies and had established a style of film humor unrivaled in the world. Even today, almost a hundred years after their initial popularity, these rollicking, wildly paced movies still delight modern audiences.

In 1938 Mack Sennett was presented with an honorary Academy Award. He died on November 5, 1960, at the age of eighty.

HOLLYWOOD'S VERY FIRST FEATURE FILM

1913

His name was Shmuel Gelbfisz when he walked across Europe from his native Poland at the age of sixteen. Soon he made it across the channel to England, then put together enough money, by one means or another, for a ship's passage across the Atlantic. He landed in Canada then headed south to New York State. In Gloversville he got a job working in a glove factory and then became a glove salesman, quickly becoming very successful at it. *Gelbfisz* was anglicized to Goldfish, and *Shmuel* became Sam.

The year was 1910, and the now-successful glove salesman met, courted, and married a young lady named Blanche Lasky. Her brother, Jesse, just happened to be a theatrical producer, and Sam Goldfish, who had by chance seen a few early films, talked to Jesse and tried to convince him that he should consider getting involved in this new popular attraction called the movies. Neither of them knew anything about moviemaking, and neither did a young playwright who had worked for Lasky. His name was Cecil B. DeMille.

It took a lot of convincing, but Lasky eventually agreed. Lasky, Goldfish, and DeMille partnered with a lawyer named Arthur Friend and, using money that Sam and Jesse put up (a total of $15,000), launched their company, the Jesse L. Lasky Feature Play Company.

The group decided early on that they did not want to make short, ten-minute films like those being shown in nickelodeons and vaudeville theaters around the country. Many theater owners even called these short films "chasers" because they effectively chased people out of the theater so they wouldn't stay and watch the vaudeville show more than once—leaving seats for another paying audience. Lasky and company wanted to make longer stories, and DeMille suggested for their first venture a play called *The Squaw Man,* which had already had some success on the New York stage. Since it was a love story but also had a western locale, they felt it would appeal to both men and women. And since it would be shot mostly outdoors, they thought it could be made cheaply. The group bought the rights from the author (Edwin Royle) for $4,000 and was able to sign up popular stage actor Dustin Farnum to headline the cast.

Then came the question as to exactly where filming should take place. Jesse Lasky suggested a location he had once visited that might have the proper feel to it: Flagstaff, Arizona. The others agreed (even though they had never been there), and in December 1913 DeMille and his minimal cast and crew boarded a train west. Lasky stayed behind to manage his theatrical business, and Sam Goldfish was still working as a glove salesman. Sam had gambled all his savings on this project, and it was a gamble he could not easily afford to lose.

Flagstaff, however, did not look at all like the West DeMille had imagined. So he decided then and there to continue west—all the way to Los Angeles. There they found a barn at the corner of Vine and Selma Streets, in what is now the heart of Hollywood. DeMille sent a telegram back to Lasky that said, "Flagstaff no good for our purpose. Have proceeded to California. Want authority to rent barn in place called Hollywood for $75 a month. Regards to Sam."

With some trepidation, Sam and Jesse agreed, but they realized the cost of the film was now beyond their company's assets. Sam, however, had learned a lot selling gloves all these years. He advertised in the newspapers the new company's prospective roster of feature-length films, and promised that their first one, *The Squaw Man,* would be an "epic of the screen" and that theater owners could charge 25 cents a ticket (rather than the 5 or 10 cents currently being charged). He also promised that movies were destined to become "the greatest entertainment medium in the world."

Sam Goldfish's promotion quickly began to work, and he was able to sell "states' rights" distribution to a wide variety of areas. What the distributors were unaware of was the fact that the money they were putting up was desperately needed to finish the first film!

DeMille, assisted by experienced director Oscar Apfel, worked assiduously filming *The Squaw Man* for the next few weeks. It was basically a simple tale of an Englishman who comes to the Wild West seeking his villainous brother, and the Indian maiden who saves his life. A romance ensues, and the Indian girl bears the man's child. Subsequently, there is a tragic ending, as she kills herself because of the shame.

DeMille invited Lasky to come out to Hollywood and see the finished film. Almost everyone connected with the production assembled in the barn (Goldfish was still on the East Coast making distribution deals to raise money). The lights were turned out and the projector was turned on, but the images jumped and crawled all over the screen. The actors appeared, then their bodies moved up and only their feet were shown. They tried again to project the print, but the result was just as disastrous.

Lasky and DeMille looked at each other. They felt that all their money was gone and, worse yet, the money their distributors had supplied was gone. All they had was a film that could not be projected, a complete and total disaster.

When Sam heard the news, he decided to go for help to the man who was perhaps the most knowledgeable person in the film business. His name was Sigmund Lubin, and he had been involved with motion pictures since their earliest days, as far back as 1896. Even though Lubin was a competitor, he agreed to look into the problem. Lasky met with DeMille, and they took a train to Lubin's office in Philadelphia. If the negative was at fault, they realized there was nothing they could do.

After Lubin looked at both the negative and the print, however, he gave them the good news: The negative was fine. The print, however, had had its sprockets punched on a British machine that punched sixty-five holes per foot, and the negative was on American film stock that had sixty-four holes per foot. Once the print was corrected, *The Squaw Man* was ready to be shown.

On February 17, 1914, at the Longacre Theater in New York, the film had its first screening. In spite of the fact that the film broke six times, the invited audience was impressed with the hour-long presentation. Sam Goldfish was now surrounded by prospective distributors who wanted to put up money to show *The Squaw Man* in their movie houses. One of these distributors was Louis B. Mayer, who offered $4,000 for the rights to show the picture in his theaters.

By the end of February, *The Squaw Man* was in release in theaters, and more and more distributors came aboard to buy the rights for their states. By spring the company Lasky and Goldfish had created had grossed almost a quarter of a million dollars.

Their company would, many years later, become Paramount Pictures. Sam Goldfish would, some years later, change his name to Sam Goldwyn. *The Squaw Man* had, however, taken its place as the very first feature-length film made in the little community of Hollywood, California.

For the Lasky Company, Sam Goldfish, and Hollywood, a lot would happen in the years that followed.

A CHARACTER IS BORN

1913

"Mack, the guy's no good!"

"What are you talkin' about?"

"The guy you just hired. You know, the Brit."

"What's the problem?"

"He's never been in a movie. Doesn't know how to act for the camera. And he does things too slow. He doesn't understand how in comedy everything is fast—a laugh every coupl'a seconds."

"Look, I saw him in a theater in New York a while back and he was hilarious."

"That was a theater. This is different."

"We just offered the guy a year's contract at $125 a week— which is about three times what Karno was payin' him. Maybe he'll improve after a while."

"Let's look at the stuff we shot yesterday."

So they did. It was a comedy they would call *Making a Living*, and the new guy wasn't very funny. The costume he was wearing made him look like a villain: The long frock coat, top hat, and drooping mustache seemed all wrong.

The two men who were talking were Henry "Pathe" Lehrman (they called him "Pathe" because he claimed to be French, and that was the name of a French film company) and Mack Sennett, who ran Keystone Studios in the community of Edendale, just a few miles from Hollywood. Sennett (who was born Michael Sinnott) had originally aspired to be a singer, but initially got involved in the movies as an actor when he noticed they were paying more than he could get singing. He worked for D. W. Griffith at Biograph for a while and learned a great deal about filmmaking. Soon he was directing his own productions and, by 1913, was able to create his own company, Keystone. Noted for their knockabout comedies, Keystone produced dozens of short films and gave the world the crazy and chaotic antics of the Keystone Kops.

Sennett had become an expert in movie slapstick comedy and had hired the British comedian, sensing he could be successful in the movies. But now he had his doubts.

Back in his tiny room, the twenty-four-year-old British actor sat brooding. He couldn't understand why he had to look at the camera. It made no sense that they photographed scenes out of order. Often they told him to look in one direction, and there was no one there to look at. He was certain he had made a mistake accepting their offer, yet $125 a week meant a lot to a young guy who had grown up in poverty, his father dead, his mother in a mental asylum. Maybe if he could just hang on, things might improve, at least for a while. He did doubt that movies would ever really catch on with the public. They were just a passing fad. People wanted to see live actors, not shadows on a screen.

It rained the next day, and the actors and crew sat around, playing cards, waiting for it to let up. Most of the shooting took place outdoors, sometimes just improvising a film from a situation like a parade that might be in progress or some other activity that might be happening on the street. So they all sat idly with little to do, since a rainstorm was quite unusual in the Los Angeles area.

The new young performer brooded as he moved around the dressing room. He looked at some trousers hanging on a hook: They belonged to the rotund comedian aptly called "Fatty" Arbuckle, who sat playing cards a few feet away.

"Mind if I—"

"Sure. Try them on if you want."

They were far too big for him, and just about everyone in the room laughed at the baggy pants.

He then saw a coat that belonged to Charlie Avery, a small man, and tried it on. It was much too tight for him, and it looked ridiculous. He found a derby hat—also too small—and popped it on his head.

There were some shoes lying round that were much too big for him, so he put them on the wrong feet and started walking in a silly shuffle. He ambled into the makeup room and found some material they used for hair. He kept trimming it down until it was just a tiny mustache, and he attached it under his nose with spirit gum. In the corner was a bamboo cane. He picked it up and started doing tricks with it, spinning it about, hooking it onto things, tipping his hat with it.

At that moment Mack Sennett came into the room and stood watching. He started to laugh.

"Hey, Chaplin!" he called. "The rain's stopped, and there's some kids' auto races down in Venice. Keep that outfit on and go with the guys."

"What's the story?"

"Just make something up."

So Charlie Chaplin, now in his new costume, headed out to make the first movie in which the "Little Tramp" would appear. And, as Sennett had suggested, they made it up as they went along. While the real cameraman cranked away, Lehrman set up a dummy camera and pointed it at the kids with their racing cars. Chaplin acted as a spectator who wandered over to see what was going on and kept getting in Lehrman's way. He used his cane as a prop, did his shuffling walk, and kept getting more and more obnoxious. And it was funny.

He appeared only for a few minutes, but the character had made its mark.

Next he showed up in a film they were making called *Mabel's Strange Predicament.* In his autobiography, Chaplin explained that he again knew little of the plot—he just wandered into the set, a hotel lobby, and, in his words, "entered and stumbled over the foot of a lady. I turned and raised my hat apologetically, then turned and stumbled over a cuspidor, then turned and raised my hat to the cuspidor. Behind the camera they began to laugh."

With some trepidation, he went to see the film at a theater in downtown Los Angeles. Though his initial bits got little response, by the time the film had ended, his comedy was getting some big laughs.

After five films, Chaplin's character had become established and he was feeling comfortable with the movie comedy business. He talked to Sennett about writing and directing his own films, but Sennett assigned him to work under the direction of Mabel Normand. Mabel was the top comedienne on the Keystone lot, and she and Sennett had also been having a longstanding romantic relationship. But Chaplin could not take her direction. He wanted to add his own style of humor, and she was not receptive to his ideas for gags.

When Sennett heard that Chaplin was refusing to work with Normand, he was furious. Chaplin felt he was about to get fired, but the next day Sennett approached the comedian with a conciliatory attitude and tried to get him to swallow his pride and work with Mabel. But Chaplin was adamant: He felt he could do better directing his own films.

"Who's going to pay for the film if we can't release the movie you make?" Sennett asked.

Chaplin took a deep breath. He had been saving almost every penny he'd earned. "I'll deposit fifteen hundred dollars in any bank. If you can't release the movie, the money is yours."

Many months later Chaplin discovered why Sennett had suddenly changed his attitude. The morning after their quarrel, Sennett had received a telegram from the New York office telling him to hurry up with more Chaplin films. The public wanted more, and the exhibitors needed many additional copies of each film to fill the demand. The Little Tramp character had made its mark and quickly touched the public's funny bone.

Chaplin would eventually make thirty-five films with Keystone, but because they would not agree to his second-year request for a much larger weekly salary, in 1916 he left Sennett's company and moved on to a studio called Essanay.

But in that first year with Keystone a character had been born, one that would soon be known to almost the entire world. It was a character Chaplin would employ over the years in a wide variety of places, times, and situations. Yet everyone would come to love and laugh with the Little Tramp as he suffered and triumphed, won and lost, charmed and annoyed in his delightful and inimitable style.

HOLLYWOOD'S FIRST FILM EPIC

1915

As the film ended and the lights came on, there was a stunned silence. Only a small group of people sat in the room, but among them was one very important man. His name was Woodrow Wilson, and he happened to be president of the United States. At first speechless, in a moment he is reported to have said, "It's like writing history with lightning." He had just seen what was, quite likely, the very first major film epic—and it would be called *The Birth of a Nation*.

The man who had made the film was David Wark Griffith. Griffith had always been a man of great aspirations. At first he wanted to achieve success as a writer, but when he got involved with the Biograph Company in New York, it was as an actor. Eventually he was given the chance to direct the ten-minute Biograph movies that were the staple of the nickelodeons that were springing up all over the country.

But Griffith was an innovator. He had his cameraman move in on the actors for close shots—something that was rarely done at that time. He experimented with unusual lighting to simulate a sunrise.

And he began to spend more time editing the films he made, often cutting back and forth between two scenes to produce dramatic tension.

Griffith soon began to feel that the ten-minute (one-reel) film was too limiting. He wanted to expand the length of film production to develop the story and the characters, to make a movie that had more of the characteristics of a book. The owners of Biograph, however, were not interested. He had made more than four hundred films in the few years he worked for them, but now it was time to move on.

Griffith's reputation was established, and he easily made a deal with the Majestic Company to supervise production of their films, and to make several each week of his own. But he wanted to do something big, and when he was shown a script for a play based on the Reverend Thomas Dixon's book *The Clansman,* he knew he had something. But first he had to convince the company to come up with the money this major production was going to cost.

Griffith met with the men in charge of Majestic, brothers Roy and Harry Aitken, to present his proposal. The film would be like no other made up to this time. It would be two hours long (twelve reels) and would encompass the sweep of the Civil War and its aftermath, the Reconstruction, telling the personal stories of families caught up in the conflict from the North and South.

The Aitkens were impressed. "How much will it cost to make?" was their critical question. "About $40,000 dollars," was Griffith's response. The brothers were shocked. Probably no film to date had cost so much. Most were made for about $1,000 per reel, and most were one or two reels long.

Yet the brothers were interested, and they took the proposal back to their board of directors. The board, however, would not agree to such a huge expenditure, so the Aitkens decided to risk their own money and monies they could raise through personal loans. They even created a separate company to make the film.

Once a deal was made with Dixon for the rights to his book, Griffith moved rapidly into production. However, since under his existing contract he was obligated to produce several short films each week for Majestic, he had to work both day and night directing the multiple projects.

Griffth made use of Dixon's plot for *The Clansman* and also another novel of his called *The Leopard's Spots.* He had sets built in Hollywood to represent the streets of the 1860s, and hired several hundred extras and put them in uniform for the sweeping Civil War battle scenes. Soon the $40,000 budget was exhausted, and when the Aitkens were unable to raise any more cash, Griffith sold shares in the production himself.

It took a year of grueling work, with Griffith working his actors and crew long hours with multiple takes and retakes. Even though there was a minimal script, the director was constantly revising and often improvising scenes when he came up with new ideas. When the shooting was finally completed, Griffith spent days and nights editing the thousands of feet of film he had shot. It was finished, at last, at a cost of $110,000.

The first public screening was on February 8, 1915, at a theater in Los Angeles called Clune's Auditorium. An orchestra was even hired to accompany the screening. Since this was a special event, Griffith felt that just a piano or organ was insufficient for such a major production—and he was right.

The audience was touched by the tender love scenes, roused by the exciting battle scenes, overwhelmed by the sheer grandeur of it all. For most of the audience, it was a totally new experience, unlike anything they had ever seen.

Author Thomas Dixon sat enthralled by the experience, and as it ended, he turned excitedly to the Aitken brothers and exclaimed, "It's better than my book—and it needs a better title. It needs to be called *The Birth of a Nation*!" And that was the title of the film from that point on.

For the picture's opening in New York, a forty-piece orchestra was hired, and Griffith worked with them for days before the screening, synchronizing their music to the film. On February 28, *The Birth of a Nation* was shown to a packed house at the Liberty Theater. The invited audience consisted of reviewers, critics, and other influential members of New York society. When it was over, there was deafening applause. Even the skeptics now realized that the motion picture could be a genuine art form and one that could arouse the deepest emotions of an audience.

The Birth of a Nation went on to become one of the highest-grossing films of its time, and it held that honor for many years. It was the first film for which theater owners charged a $2 admission—an amazing price at a time (1915) when an entire week's salary for many workers might be $5 or $10 and a person could buy a complete restaurant dinner for a single dollar!

The film earned its backers and exhibitors huge profits. Thomas Dixon, the author of the book, took a lower fee for the rights in exchange for a percentage of profits, and would ultimately make more than half a million dollars. The film did, however, generate a great deal of controversy in many circles, since it portrayed the Ku Klux Klan as a heroic group saving the South and showed the freed slaves as manipulated by the carpetbaggers who came from the North. There were even boycotts and angry newspaper articles protesting the negative portrayal of the freed slaves after the war. *The Birth of a Nation* nevertheless established D. W. Griffith's reputation as a master film director, and it would be followed by other successes—but also several major failures.

Unfortunately, time would pass Griffith by, and he died in 1948 poor and embittered by an industry that he had helped achieve prestige and artistic importance. But it was an industry that hardly remembered all he had contributed.

With *The Birth of a Nation,* D. W. Griffith had taken a giant step toward making film what it would ultimately become—perhaps the greatest dramatic medium of modern times.

THE GREATEST FILM OR THE BIGGEST FLOP?

1916

David Wark Griffith was ecstatic. His gamble had paid off. All the money and time and effort he had lavished on his great epic production, *The Birth of a Nation,* was now bearing fruit. All over the country patrons were lining up—often paying as much as $2 per ticket—to see his sweeping saga of the Civil War and its aftermath. Even the negative responses, because of his favorable depiction of the infamous Ku Klux Klan, were getting him publicity.

As the money rolled in, everyone involved in the production was happy—especially his investors. It was only natural that his next project should be of epic proportions. And it certainly would be.

The new film would encompass not one, but four stories, each intertwined with the other. All would deal with a subject that was pervasive in human history: intolerance. There would be a modern story (which he had already been working on), depicting the many indignities heaped on a poor but honest couple. There would be a sequence showing the massacre of the French Huguenots in 1572, and a vivid series of scenes of the crucifixion of Jesus. Finally, there would be an exciting tale of the fall of Babylon in the sixth century BC. And it would all be on a massive scale.

For the Babylon story he had a huge set constructed where Sunset and Hollywood Boulevards now converge. Walls almost as high as a twelve-story building, and sturdy enough to support the chariots that moved along them, were built, along with a mile-long interior courtyard. The entire set encompassed a ten-acre tract of land in Hollywood.

Carpenters, painters, and plasterers were hired. Griffith's prop master, Ralph DeLacey, began building and collecting thousands of props: furniture, swords, guns, and livestock. As many as four thousand extras were hired for the battle scenes (many from Los Angeles's skid row) and paid $2 a day. In some of the battle scenes, quite a few extras got a bit carried away, and sixty-seven ended up needing first aid for their wounds.

The costs quickly began to escalate. Griffith, however, was the only one who knew what was happening, since the whole idea was in his head and there had never been an actual script. All he had to work from were some notes and research material he had read.

For a dramatic shot that introduced the facade of the Babylonian Palace, he considered shooting from a hot-air balloon, but the balloon proved to be too unsteady for the camera. Instead they constructed a tall, rolling platform with an elevator so the camera could be moved both horizontally and vertically (probably the first use of such a device). The platform was used in a most effective way in the scene of the "Feast of Belshazzar." With thousands of extras and dancers, the camera moves in from several hundred feet away and descends, ending with a close shot.

The Babylonian scenes are perhaps the most lavish, but the modern story (which was originally to be called "The Mother and the Law") is the most exciting, since Griffith makes superb use of his rapid crosscutting (quickly going back and forth between two scenes) at the end to make it dramatically suspenseful. The basic story is of "The Boy" and "The Dear One" (most of the characters are not given names) who fall in love and marry. The Boy had previously engaged in petty crime, but after marrying the Dear One, he attempts to lead an honest life. But the crook he previously worked for, "The Musketeer of the Slums," plants stolen goods on him, and he is sent to jail. After his release, a series of events result in the shooting of the Musketeer and the false implication of the Boy as the murderer. He is on the verge of being sent to the gallows when his wife and a sympathetic police officer get a confession from the real killer and race to catch a speeding train to get the governor to issue a stay, then rush to the prison to prevent the hanging just as the Boy has ascended the gallows.

The Christ story is basically three sequences and concludes with the crucifixion.

The third story concerns a wealthy Protestant family in sixteenth-century France that is planning the marriage of their daughter, and the growing hatred of Protestant Huguenots by the Catholic Catherine de Medici. On the eve of the wedding, Catherine convinces her son, King Charles IX, to issue a decree to kill the Protestants. The climax is the St. Bartholomew's Day massacre and the slaughter of thousands of innocent people.

The most lavish story (which Griffith filmed last) made use of the massive Babylonian set. It involves the peace-loving Babylonians and their king Belshazzar, a jealous high priest, and the assault on their city by the Persians. This results in a climactic battle and the deaths of most of the principal characters.

The four stories are tied together by scenes of actress Lillian Gish sitting and rocking a cradle, based on a line from poet Walt Whitman: "Out of the cradle, endlessly rocking, uniter of here and hereafter."

The conclusion of *Intolerance* is a strange and idealistic concept. Soldiers in vicious combat are stopped by angels who appear above and stop them from killing; a high prison wall seems to vanish and the prisoners move to freedom; children play happily in a meadow while behind them the weapons of war are overgrown with flowers; and a caption says, "And Perfect Love shall bring peace forevermore." Finally, we again see the woman rocking the cradle before the image fades out.

Griffith's first cut of the film ran eight hours. He considered that he could edit it to about four hours and then release it in two parts, but the exhibitors balked at this idea. Eventually he was able to get it down to under three hours for the first showing.

Though the actual cost of the production is not known, many have speculated that it cost as much as $2 million, and this figure was widely publicized. However, author Richard Schickel, in his book on Griffith, has done a careful analysis of all available material, and he believes the most accurate figure is slightly less than $400,000. Even this figure, though, in 1916 would equal many millions in modern dollars.

In any event, the costs escalated rapidly throughout production, and Griffith as well as some of his actors put their own money into the picture, feeling secure that it, like *The Birth of a Nation,* would be a solid moneymaker. But, unfortunately, it was not to be.

Griffith had made the film to show how intolerance has pervaded the world through many different epochs, thus the film concludes with that paean for universal peace and understanding to combat the forces of intolerance in the world. But just a few months after the film opened in April 1917, the United States declared war on Germany and entered World War I. The peace message of *Intolerance* was no longer appealing to a now-militant public.

In addition, many people who saw the film were confused and could not deal with the complex amalgamation of four stories and the constant shifting from one to the other. Even the *New York Times* reviewer called it "interesting" and "unusual," but then referred to the picture's "utter incoherence" and "questionable taste."

Although *Intolerance* did well in its initial screenings in major cities, its audience soon fell off. Unlike *The Birth of a Nation,* word of mouth did not make it a "must-see" experience for the audiences of 1917. Perhaps it was a film that was simply ahead of its time. It would, however, have a major influence on a later breed of film directors who would copy many of Griffith's techniques and study his directorial innovations.

In his excellent study, *D. W. Griffith: An American Life,* Richard Schickel asserts that it was not World War I nor the complexity of the story that harmed the film, but the fact that the director's shifting from one story to another did not allow the audience the opportunity to identify with the characters. For him, *Intolerance* is "an easy film to respect, but a hard film to cherish."

Intolerance has, through the years, been seen as a major milestone in the development of film as an art. It was, however, a financial flop, and unfortunately Hollywood then—as now—equated success with box office revenues. To many it was a film that broke new ground in its technique, and a high point in Griffith's career. But it did not help the director's reputation at the time, and he would ever after be the man who made prestigious films, but not films that made a profit.

HOUDINI'S GREAT ESCAPE—
TO HOLLYWOOD

1919

A poor, defenseless young lady lies tied to the railroad tracks as a train speeds toward her prostrate body.

A handsome young man is trapped in a cabin that has been set afire by savages.

Another young damsel is in a tiny boat that is suddenly caught in some rapids and is headed for a raging waterfall.

These were the scenes that would often end an episode of a movie serial. Audiences would have to wait for the next week's episode to find out just how the leading characters would be extricated from these seemingly impossible dilemmas.

Perhaps the most famous performer in these serials was Pearl White, who gained notoriety in her series *The Perils of Pauline.* But in 1919 another well-known performer decided to try his hand at being in the movies, and to perform in a serial. He was widely known for his achievements in another area, but he was always eager to try new things.

His name was Harry Houdini.

Born in Budapest, Hungary, in 1874 but raised in Appleton, Wisconsin, Ehrich Weiss started performing magic tricks when he was a child. When he read a book by the famous French magician Robert-Houdin, he decided to add an *i* to the magician's name, and since he was often called "Ehrie" (which sounded like "Harry"), he adopted this as well. In short order he became Harry Houdini.

Houdini began his career working hard as a performer in fairs and dime museums for just a few dollars a day. But when a booking agent noticed him doing a handcuff escape, his career began to take off. In 1899 he was booked on a vaudeville circuit—mainly as an escape artist—and a year later Houdini and his wife took a chance and set sail for Europe. In England, Germany, and Russia he accepted a variety of challenges and escaped from chains, handcuffs, manacles, and even the local prisons. He was a sensation.

Over the years Houdini's reputation grew rapidly, and soon he was in demand everywhere. By 1919, when he was forty-five years old, the strain of doing the many challenging escapes, as well as the constant touring, had become wearing, so he was happy to take advantage of a major acting role in the serial *The Master Mystery.* True to the typical serial format, the fifteen episodes gave Houdini a chance to escape from a straitjacket, manacles, and a diving suit; fight his way to the surface after being immersed in gravel; and escape from a jail cell and get loose from the straps holding him in an electric chair. Other episodes of the serial had him extricating himself while tied at the bottom of an elevator shaft as the descending elevator moved closer and closer to crushing him, and untangling himself from barbed wire before a flow of acid burned his body.

Despite breaking some bones in his wrist (he did all the stunts himself), once filming was completed, he was back to doing his escapes on the theater stage. But Houdini was bitten by the movie bug, and in 1919 he signed a contract to star in a feature film to be made in Hollywood by Paramount-Artcraft Pictures called *The Grim Game*. Once again the script called for a host of daredevil stunts for the escapist to perform, and once again he was up to the challenge.

In this film he broke out of a jail cell and also escaped from a straitjacket while hanging upside down. The script also called for him to make a transfer from one airplane to another while they were in flight. During the filming the two planes collided, became entangled, and ended up crash-landing in a bean field. Fortunately no one was seriously injured. A third plane filmed the action, and the footage was eventually used in the movie and given lots of publicity. What was not divulged, however, was that Houdini was not in either plane. His arm was in a sling, since he had refractured his delicate left wrist when he fell a mere three feet in the jail cell escape. The stuntman in one plane had taken all the risks, but Houdini took all the credit—he even told a magazine interviewer that the crash had almost amputated his limbs. One thing he was never ashamed to do was hype his exploits.

Reviewers called *The Grim Game* "jammed full of thrills" and "an avalanche of sensational feats which chill the marrow." Houdini reveled in the acclaim and enjoyed his time in Hollywood. Among the many stars he got to know were Charlie Chaplin and famed actress Gloria Swanson. He even had himself photographed hand-cuffing director Cecil B. DeMille. He quickly signed with Famous Players–Lasky to do a second production called *Terror Island*.

Filmed mostly on Catalina Island (off the Southern California coast), the plot of *Terror Island* involved the recovery of diamonds from a sunken ship and the rescue of the father of the heroine (played by Lila Lee) from some island savages. The film lacked the thrilling escapes of *The Grim Game* and had a host of improbable scenes: In one sequence the heroine is stuffed into a safe and thrown off a cliff into the sea, yet Houdini finds the safe and frees her.

Probably more exciting than the film was an event that occurred that almost cost Houdini his life. One day before production, a small boat containing four film crew members was hit by high waves and was in danger of being wrecked on the rocks. Houdini saw what was happening, lashed a line around his waist, put a life preserver over his head, and started to swim to the boat in the icy water. But the rough sea was too much for him and, battered and bleeding, he had to be brought back by some deep-sea divers. The boat was eventually rescued by a motor launch that had to fight the surf for forty-five minutes to reach the imperiled craft.

Regardless of the real-life heroics, reviews of *Terror Island* were hardly glowing. The show business periodical *Billboard* wrote that some scenes "caused the audience to laugh outright." And *Variety* said that the only reason for *Terror Island* was as an excuse to bring Houdini back to the screen.

Meanwhile, Houdini had started his own film-processing plant and would soon create his own production company, but by assuming virtually all the jobs—including star, director, writer, and producer—he was obviously taking on too much responsibility. Over the next few years he would make two more feature films, but both proved disastrous. *The Man from Beyond* has the weird plot of a man (Houdini) who has been encased in ice for a century and is brought back to life. There are only a few exciting moments—especially the final sequence where the heroine is saved from going over Niagara Falls by Houdini. But even with Houdini appearing in person at screenings throughout the country and performing a stage show of magic and escapes, it would still prove to be a financial failure.

His last film, *Haldane of the Secret Service,* had him playing the role of a Secret Service agent. It, too, failed to score with audiences. When a small crowd showed up for the film's premiere, *Variety* reported, "Perhaps the renown of Houdini is fading. . . . With all due respect to his famed ability for escapes, the only asset he has in the acting line is his ability to look alert."

Houdini lost considerable money in these later film ventures, and they proved to be his final assaults on moviedom. He went back to performing, in addition to starting a major campaign to expose fraudulent mediums who preyed on gullible people hoping to make contact with their lost loved ones.

His tragic (and some consider strange) death occurred on Halloween 1926, the result of several stomach punches by a college student that ruptured his appendix. Despite the severe pain, he continued to perform, but soon was forced to enter the hospital. Even two surgeries, however, could not stop the infection (there were no antibiotics at the time), and he died at the age of fifty-two of peritonitis.

Houdini's brief foray into cinema is not one of the activities he would be most noted for, yet it remains a record of some of the exploits of the great magician.

MABEL, MARY, AND MURDER

1922

On February 1, 1922, Henry Peavey arrived for work at his employer's bungalow in the Westlake Park area of Los Angeles, not far from Hollywood. Peavey was the butler and general factotum to the Hollywood director William Desmond Taylor.

On the floor lay his employer, and a single .38-caliber bullet wound was later discovered in his back. Taylor was just a few months short of his fiftieth birthday.

Peavey's first call was to friends of Taylor's, and by the time the police arrived, numerous people were in the bungalow and a great deal of potential evidence had been compromised. And much like a movie, there were several aspects of Taylor's life that had been kept secret and, not surprisingly, many people in his life who had strong motives to want him dead.

Taylor's real name was William Cunningham Deane Tanner, and he was born in Carlow, Ireland, probably in 1872. In 1890 he came to the United States and, because of his charm and good looks, sought out a career in the theater. He was somewhat successful in getting a few small parts in Broadway shows, but then in 1901 he met Ethel May Harrison and the two were married. Soon the couple had a daughter, Ethel Daisy, and his wife's wealthy father set William up with an antiques shop in New York. However, not long after, he began drinking heavily, as well as seeing other women.

It seems the life of an antiques dealer, even with a 1902 salary of $29,000 a year, did not satisfy William, and on October 23, 1908, he simply vanished, walking out on his wife, daughter, and antiques shop, telling no one where he was going.

For the next few years he took on a wide variety of jobs: hotel manager in Colorado, prospecting in the Klondike, touring with a traveling acting company. He also took on a new name, William Desmond Taylor, and, in 1912, arrived in Hollywood. Once again, his good looks worked for him. He was cast in some minor movie roles, and in 1914 was given a starring role in a film called *Captain Alvarez.*

It wasn't long before he was given an opportunity to direct, and in this position, Taylor found his place. In 1915 he directed a serial called *The Diamond from the Sky* and was soon put in charge of feature films that included *Tom Sawyer* (1917), *Anne of Green Gables* (1919), and *Huckleberry Finn* (1920). Among the well-known actresses he directed were Mary Pickford and Mary Miles Minter. By 1922 he had directed more than thirty major productions.

Taylor, however, apparently had a penchant for starlets, and one of these was the young Minter. Born Juliet Reilly in 1902, she was given the name Mary Miles Minter by her mother, Charlotte Shelby, who constantly pushed her to become a successful actress. Shelby had used her deceased niece's birth certificate to "prove" her daughter was old enough to work full-time in a show in Chicago. The birth certificate contained the name Mary Miles Minter, which her daughter would use from then on.

By 1915 Charlotte Shelby realized the real money for her actress-daughter was in the movies, so she negotiated a deal first with Metro Pictures, then with Flying A. With young Mary's popularity rapidly growing with each film, she was ultimately signed with Paramount Pictures at the amazing sum of $1.3 million.

In addition to his dalliance with Mary, Taylor had also had an extensive relationship with Mabel Normand. Normand, born in 1892, made her film debut with D. W. Griffith when he was at Biograph. At Biograph she met Mack Sennett, and when he set up his own studio, Keystone, in 1912, Mabel went along. Over the years she and Sennett had an on-again, off-again romantic relationship. She was a skillful and popular comedienne and made many successful films with such performers as Charlie Chaplin, Marie Dressler, and Roscoe "Fatty" Arbuckle. In 1916 she even set up her own studio (The Mabel Normand Feature Film Company). Normand was attracted to Taylor because he was literate and urbane, in contrast to the more rough-hewn Sennett.

Among the other characters involved in this complex tale was Edward Sands, a man Taylor had hired as his personal secretary and chauffeur. Less than a year before Taylor's death, while the director was in Europe, Sands had disappeared, taking with him money, jewelry, and an expensive automobile that belonged to his employer.

Then there was Charlotte Shelby, Mary Miles Minter's controlling mother, who had recently discovered that her daughter had an infatuation with Taylor and was incensed—she was even known to own a .38-caliber revolver. There were also rumors that she was secretly in love with Taylor.

Neighbors gave the police some information about the night of the murder. They claimed they had heard a gunshot between 7:45 and 8:15 that night, and a person wearing a cap and overcoat had been observed leaving Taylor's bungalow.

Although the murder was never solved, film director King Vidor had long wanted to make a film about the Taylor case. He was also determined to discover the identity of the killer.

In 1967 (more than forty years after the murder), Vidor embarked on an extensive investigation, doing numerous interviews and tracking down any information that was still available.

For various reasons he chose not to make the film, but after Vidor's death in 1982, his biographer, Sidney Kirkpatrick, was able to reconstruct the investigation. Kirkpatrick's book, *A Cast of Killers* (published in 1986), goes over the details of the case, and his conclusion is that Charlotte Shelby was the one who pulled the trigger. Based on what he learned, Mary Miles Minter had gone to Taylor's bungalow the night of the murder, and her mother had followed her there. Shelby wore a cap and long coat to conceal her identity, and it was she, not a man, who was very likely the person seen by the neighbors leaving the area. Shelby's alibi, supported by both her daughters (Mary and Margaret), was that they were all home together on that fateful night. Charlotte Shelby was never charged.

The lives of many of the people involved with William Desmond Taylor would suffer one way or another after his death. Mary Miles Minter made just four films after the murder and then retired from the screen, saying that she had never really been happy as an actress. In 1925 she sued her mother for money she felt she had not received during her career as a child star, and the case was settled out of court. Minter died in 1984 from a stroke at the age of eighty. Her star on the Hollywood Walk of Fame is located on Vine Street.

Mabel Normand made two feature films after Taylor's death: *Suzanna* and *The Extra Girl,* both in 1923. Shortly after, her chauffeur shot and injured an oil millionaire named Courtland Dines. The gun he used was registered in Normand's name. Though she was not implicated, her acting career sputtered to a halt, and she only made a few short films for the Hal Roach Studios in 1926. In 1928 she was diagnosed with tuberculosis and admitted to Pottenger Sanitarium in Monrovia, California. Throughout much of her life she had been a heavy drinker, and it was rumored that she had been a drug user as well. She died in February 1930 at the age of thirty-seven.

Charlotte Shelby reconciled with her daughter Mary and reportedly died in March 1957. However, rumor had it that she was not dead and had been seen living with Mary as late as 1980.

Henry Peavey, who had been Taylor's butler and discovered his body, moved to Sacramento after the murder and apparently lived in poverty. He made statements to the press in 1930 that Taylor had been killed by a famous actress and her mother, but he had been told to keep quiet about it. He died in 1937.

The Taylor murder was just one of numerous scandals that rocked Hollywood in the twenties, making it partly responsible for the massive public outcry that initiated the creation of the Hays Office, which resulted in heavy censorship of movie content. This censorship would last for many years to come and would sharply restrict the language and the material of hundreds of films that were made throughout the thirties, forties, and fifties.

MR. HAYS SAYS "NO!"

1922

Sex! Violence! Obscenity! Profanity! Prostitution! Adultery!

The movies, said many, were replete with all of the above. They advertised titles like *A Shocking Night, Virgin Paradise, Husbands and Lovers, Paid to Love, Charming Sinners, Faithless,* and *Call Her Savage.* Even worse, the behavior of those in Hollywood went far beyond the bounds of normal propriety.

The newspapers duly reported the murder of William Desmond Taylor and his possible love affairs with both Mabel Normand and young starlet Mary Miles Minter. Rotund funnyman Roscoe "Fatty" Arbuckle was put on trial for the rape of a young woman at a wild party. The woman had subsequently died, but after several trials, Arbuckle was found innocent. Charming leading man Wallace Reid had died of influenza at the age of thirty-one, his body weakened by alcohol and morphine addiction.

Movie censorship had been around almost since the first films appeared, and as early as 1911 Pennsylvania created a state board of censors. Numerous other states did likewise. However, rising public opinion about Hollywood and its shameful products stimulated the film producers to do something before the government did something first. Founded in March 1922, the Motion Picture Producers and Distributors of America (MPPDA) quickly chose a man of impeccable credentials to be its president.

William Harrison Hays was forty-three years old and was a Presbyterian deacon and a staunch Republican. He had even managed the successful presidential campaign of Warren G. Harding in 1920. In exchange, Harding had appointed him to the cabinet post of postmaster general. But now Hollywood beckoned—not to mention a yearly salary of $100,000 (more than that of the president!).

Hays's appointment was widely publicized, and it was reported that his job would be to "clean up the movies." But the position really had little in the way of actual censorship power, since the studios were just being advised to police themselves, and Hays would merely be given synopses of material the producers were considering making. His job would be to advise the studios about the content. In addition, Hays made a list of existing books and plays (many of them Broadway hits) that would be prohibited material.

By 1926 Hays had compiled a list of what he called "Don'ts and Be Carefuls." The "Don'ts" included subjects like licentious nudity, illegal drug traffic, sex perversion, and ridicule of the clergy. The "Be Carefuls" were subjects that had to be handled with special care, like the use of firearms, robbery, brutality, the sale of women, men and women in bed together, and lustful kissing. Yet these were still only advisory, and many producers ignored them.

Along came Martin Quigley, publisher of the *Motion Picture Herald,* and Daniel Lord, a drama teacher at St. Louis University. With Hays's agreement, they drew up the famous (or infamous) Production Code. This elaborate document, more than four thousand words in length, detailed the standards for films to follow. Adopted by the producers in March of 1930, it contained such statements as "No picture shall be produced which will lower the moral standards of those who see it" and "Law—divine, natural, or human—shall not be ridiculed, nor shall sympathy be created for its violation."

It then proceeded to list dozens of "thou shalt nots" that included:

- Methods of crime shall not be explicitly presented.

- There shall be no scenes of law-enforcing officers dying at the hands of criminals.

- Adultery and illicit sex . . . shall not be explicitly treated.

- Sex perversion or any inference of it is forbidden.

- Vulgar expressions and double meanings having the same effect are forbidden.

- Profanity is forbidden.

- Indecent or undue exposure is forbidden.

The code went on and on in detail explaining all the items to be forbidden, avoided, or treated with great care. Yet despite the producers' agreeing to it (or perhaps really paying lip service to it), not a great deal changed.

Then in April 1934, the Roman Catholic Church convened a meeting of the Committee of Bishops. Among the subjects they discussed was the content of motion pictures and the lives and habits of the people who worked in Hollywood. From their discussion they created the Legion of Decency, and what this Legion of Decency did was to watch and evaluate the content of virtually every feature film. They created six categories that included acceptable for all

(A-I), for adults and adolescents (A-II), for adults only (A-III), and for adults—with reservations (A-IV). There was a rating of B for films morally objectionable in part for all, but if the Legion believed the content was totally offensive, they branded the film C for "Condemned." This label was enough to get Catholics all over the country to refuse to attend.

To the studio moguls who made the films, this tactic sent shivers of fear down their spines. They were terrified of losing business, and even more significant, since the studios at this time owned the theaters that showed the films, a threatened boycott of individual theaters could be disastrous to box office receipts. So, in June 1934, the producers adopted a resolution agreeing to abide by the Production Code, requiring a seal of approval on the films and a $25,000 fine for infractions.

By 1940 Will Hays was boasting that 95 percent of the theaters in America showed only the films that had the seal. The studios had successfully avoided government censorship by developing their own system.

Hays put a Catholic journalist named Joseph Breen in charge of reviewing proposed scripts that were submitted to his office for evaluation, and Breen exercised his power with vigor. In his hands stories with bedroom scenes became stories with patio scenes, prostitutes morphed into dancers, and double beds (even for married couples) were changed to twin beds. Forbidden were words like "madam," "pansy," "tart," and even "nuts." It was considered blasphemous for a character to say "Oh, God!" and writers were told not to use the phrase. Childbirth was not to be shown, which proved to be a challenge in a crucial scene in *Gone With the Wind*, and not many years later in *From Here to Eternity*, a prostitute became a bar waitress.

The Hays Office was diligent in its scrutiny: First they looked at any book or play a studio was considering and made an evaluation of its suitability to become a film; then they went over the script and made comments about individual scenes, dialogue, and even implied or suggestive content; and finally they looked at the finished movie and often forced producers to cut or change scenes already shot.

From 1934 all the way to 1968, the Hays Office ruled the content of movies, and filmmakers had to come up with ways to phrase things or circumvent the stranglehold of the Code. By the fifties, however, there was a relaxation of standards, and film producers began to get away with scenes that never would have made it by the censors just ten years before. Once again the reason was not morality, but money.

Two major events happened that changed things: First, television reared its head, and audiences attracted to this novelty were easily lured away from the big screen to the small one; and second, a court decision forced the major film companies to divest themselves of theater ownership (since this was considered monopolistic). Now films without the Code's seal of approval could be shown, and foreign films and motion pictures made by independent producers had a chance of having an audience. Even the Hays Office began to relax its restrictions.

Finally, in 1968, the days of the Hays Office ended. (Will Hays himself had died in 1954.) Jack Valenti had become president of the Motion Picture Association of America in 1966, and he, along with others in the industry, felt that change was necessary, and a rating system was put into place.

The original rating system established in 1968 has undergone several changes. With the current G/PG/PG-13/R/NC-17 system, moviemakers can make virtually any kind of film they want. But, of course, money still dictates content, and censorship (of a slightly different variety) remains. Today the ideal rating is perhaps PG-13, since it allows anyone to attend but suggests "parental guidance."

Many aspects of the movies changed when Mr. Hays first said "No!" Yet even today, when it seems as though almost anything can find its way to the movie screen, the successors of Will Hays, who currently determine the ratings of films, continue to exercise a considerable degree of power over the motion pictures that find their way onto the screens of America's theaters.

"YOU AIN'T HEARD NOTHIN' YET!"

1927

It was one of the most popular Broadway shows of the twenties, and its star was comedian and singer George Jessel. Based on the magazine story "The Day of Atonement" by Samson Raphaelson, it was about the son of a Jewish cantor who, despite his father's expectations, chooses not to follow in the family footsteps, but instead leaves to attempt a career as a popular singer.

Years pass, and the father becomes ill and unable to sing on the eve of the Jewish High Holiday of Yom Kippur. The young man's mother seeks him out and implores him to sing the famous "Kol Nidre" hymn that initiates Yom Kippur. But the boy has been cast in a Broadway show, and that night will be the show's opening. Torn between his obligations to his career and to his family, the young man finally chooses to leave the show (despite the possible repercussions) and sing the "Kol Nidre."

The show based on Raphaelson's story was called *The Jazz Singer,* and the film studio that bought the rights to adapt it for the screen was not one of the major players in Hollywood. It was, by many standards, a second-rate production company that had been formed by four brothers: Harry, Sam, Albert, and Jack Warner. It was also a company that was constantly low on cash, so the $50,000 they paid for the rights to make a film of *The Jazz Singer* was definitely a major investment.

There was, however, something else they had in mind.

Several systems of sound films had evolved over the years, but most of the major studios had resisted investing in them. They felt they were too costly, merely a fad, totally unnecessary (printed titles provided most dialogue), and would prove a problem with non-English-speaking audiences. But Harry Warner believed that the future of the movies was in sound, and his studio had already produced some short films with musical accompaniment as well as the feature picture *Don Juan,* which was accompanied by a full orchestral score.

The sound system was the Vitaphone system, which utilized a wax disc and cue sheets for the projectionist to keep it synchronized. The Warners knew it would be a risky decision—as well as a potentially expensive one—but they felt the public was ready.

They approached George Jessel, who had starred in the stage play, and made him an offer to repeat the role in the film. Although versions of the story differ, Jessel finally turned down the part, either because he and Harry Warner could not agree on his salary, or, as Jessel claimed, he was unhappy with the rewriting that had been done to the original script, especially the ending.

The Warners next offered the part to singer/comedian Eddie Cantor, but he also said no.

Their third choice was singer Al Jolson. Interestingly, *The Jazz Singer* bore a strong resemblance to Jolson's real life (in fact, Jolson may well have been the inspiration for the Raphaelson story). Born in Russia in 1888, Asa Yoelson (his real name) was brought to the

United States as a small child. His father wanted him to follow in the family footsteps and become a cantor in the synagogue, but the young man rebelled and ran away from home. Desperately eager to perform in the theater, he worked first in circuses, then in cafes, and ultimately became a singer in vaudeville. In 1906 he put on blackface and sang with a Southern accent. Soon he became a very popular Broadway performer, and his renditions of songs like "Mammy," "Sonny Boy," and "Swanee" endeared him to audiences and made him a highly successful singer.

When Jolson was contacted by Warner Brothers to appear in *The Jazz Singer,* he had already made some short films, and even sang "April Showers" in one brief sound film that the company had made. Jolson asked for $75,000 to do the film. The Warners agreed, and in August 1927 Al Jolson stepped onto the newly soundproofed stage at Warner Brothers Studio on Sunset Boulevard in Hollywood to begin production of what would become a groundbreaking motion picture.

Making a sound film in 1927, however, proved to be an experience much different from what filmmaking had been in the past. With silent films the director could talk his actors through a scene, mood music might be played in the background (romantic tunes to put the actors in the right mood for a love scene, tense minor chords to create dramatic moments), and there was often the chatter of the crew, the crackle of arc lights, and the sounds of set-building somewhere in the studio.

But all this changed when sound had to be recorded. The walls and floor were lined with soundproofing material, and doors were kept tightly closed. Visitors to the set found they were prohibited from entering during "takes" by flashing red lights outside the doors. The cameras were contained in tightly sealed booths (that would get unbearably hot), and filming was done through plate-glass windows, making camera mobility all but impossible. There was a monitoring room for the sound man and a playback room to listen to the just-recorded scenes. And to make the actors' lives more difficult, the microphones were often hidden behind objects on tables, making the performers extremely limited in their ability to move around.

The Jazz Singer, however, had been scripted to incorporate mostly printed titles for the majority of the dialogue, and the emphasis had been to only record sound when Jolson sang. But in one scene, after he sings "Dirty Hands, Dirty Face" and gets applause, Jolson says, "Wait a minute . . . wait a minute. You ain't heard nothin' yet," then launches into a favorite song of his called "Toot, Toot, Tootsie." These few spoken words hit audiences like a bombshell. They were, probably, the very first spoken words uttered in a feature film, and it all might have happened accidentally. Still later in the film, there is a brief, humorous dialogue scene between Jolson and his mother.

On October 6, 1927, the film opened in New York at the Warners Theater. For the Warner brothers, it was a huge gamble and had cost them half a million dollars. If it failed, it might well have meant an end to their careers in the motion picture business.

Al Jolson, with great trepidation, attended the premiere, but his fears proved to be totally unfounded. When THE END flashed on the screen, the audience rose in wild applause, and Jolson, with tears in his eyes, took a bow.

One of the Warners was not present for their moment of triumph, however. On October 5 Harry, Albert, and Jack had rushed to the bedside of brother Sam. Just a day before the premiere, Sam had died of a brain abscess, complicated by pneumonia.

Reviews of the film proved to be laudatory, for the most part. The *New York Times* reviewer said that "not since the first presentation of Vitaphone features . . . has anything like the ovation been heard in a motion-picture theater." The show business newspaper

Variety wrote that the film was "the best thing Vitaphone has ever put on the screen." However, the *Los Angeles Times* headline read, "'Jazz Singer' Scores a Hit—Vitaphone and Al Jolson Responsible, Picture Itself Second Rate."

The public responded to the new experience enthusiastically, and *The Jazz Singer* was one of the top-grossing pictures of the year. Not long afterwards, the other studios, now finally convinced that the future was in sound films, made deals with Western Electric's licensing division, ERPI (Electrical Research Products, Inc.), for conversion to sound. By mid-1928 three hundred theaters had been wired for sound-film presentation, and by the end of that year it was estimated that a thousand movie theaters would be ready for the new experience.

Warners quickly completed *Lights of New York,* a musical crime drama, that would take its place as the first all-talking feature film. Over the ensuing years, Warner Brothers would become one of Hollywood's biggest studios, with a long list of major productions and stars and a name that would be recognized by moviegoers around the world.

Al Jolson would go on to make numerous films, including *The Singing Fool* (1928), one of the biggest moneymakers for Warners; *Sonny Boy* (1929); *Say It With Songs* (1929); and *Mammy* (1930). All were touching and sentimental, and all utilized Jolson performing his popular repertoire. He went on to make several additional films in the thirties, but by 1940 he had returned to the stage.

During World War II Jolson sang to American troops, regaining his popularity and giving Columbia Studios the idea to do a movie about his life. Jolson was unhappy that they cast Larry Parks to play him, but he was fifty-eight years old at the time, and the studio wanted a new, younger face. His voice was used for the songs, and Parks mimed the singing. *The Jolson Story* (1946) was a rather ordinary backstage-type movie but proved to be a huge success, and Jolson became popular once again on radio and recordings. Columbia followed it with *Jolson Sings Again* (1949), picking up his life story where the first film had ended.

Al Jolson died in 1950 at the age of sixty-two, a man who had had many careers, but would always be known for his groundbreaking appearance in the film that changed everything: *The Jazz Singer.*

THE GREAT AERIAL EPIC

1927

The man behind the desk was furious. He seethed with anger when he heard the news. But he vowed not only to get even, but to do it in the most dramatic way he could afford—and he could afford almost anything. The man was the eccentric billionaire Howard Hughes, and his anger was over the rights to a movie called *Wings* that his friend, John Monk Saunders, had sold to Paramount Studios.

Born in Humble, Texas, in 1905, Howard Hughes had inherited a fortune from his father, who had developed a drill bit for the oil-drilling industry and founded an enterprise called Hughes Tool Company. But young Howard was more interested in the movies and wanted to make a name for himself as a film producer. He loved to hobnob with Hollywood personalities—especially the attractive young starlets. He was also fascinated with flying, and this made him especially angry when the rights to *Wings* went to Paramount.

He decided he would make his own aerial epic.

Hughes had already produced several films, and some had shown success, but he wanted to embark on a project that would be large and sweeping in scope, so he hired writer/director Marshall Neilan to develop a script based on an idea Neilan had suggested to him. It was a World War I story of two brothers, both of whom were infatuated with the same young woman, but it would include lots of combat action—especially in the air. It would be called *Hell's Angels*.

Hughes also realized that if he wanted to make a picture about flying, he had to learn to fly himself, so he began taking lessons at Clover Field, west of Los Angeles. He knew that to command respect from the flyers he was about to hire for the film, he had to be conversant with all aspects of planes and the piloting of them.

He was just twenty-three years old at the time, but his company was doing well, so he started buying and renovating airplanes, ultimately spending over half a million dollars on them. He hired a well-known stunt flyer named Frank Tomick to obtain all the aircraft he could find for the film—all on an open budget.

Hughes also hired thirty-five cameramen, many of whom were skilled in aerial photography, and acquired some of the nation's top stunt flyers. One of the cameramen was Harry Perry, an expert in shooting aerial scenes and a technician who had developed cameras and camera mounts to solve the numerous problems encountered while filming in the air.

Because the script for *Hell's Angels* called for locations in England and Germany, many of the aircraft they acquired needed to be repainted and redesigned to simulate British and German planes. Airfields were also needed, so Hughes bought a cow pasture in Van Nuys, north of Los Angeles, and named it Caddo Field. There they built hangars and other buildings. Hughes reveled in all the activity and supervised much of the construction himself. He also bought land in Inglewood, south and west of Los Angeles. This land would, years later, become the site of Los Angeles International Airport. In the far western part of the San Fernando Valley (a community now known as Chatsworth), he bought property that would become the German air base.

Hughes chose topflight actors to play the leading roles: Ben Lyon and James Hall for the brothers, and Norwegian actress Greta Nissen as the love interest. Since it was to be a silent film, he was not concerned with Nissen's thick Scandinavian accent.

On October 31, 1927, filming began, but Hughes quickly became unhappy with his chosen director, Luther Reed, and took over directing the film himself. During the shooting of the aerial sequences, Hughes put heavy demands on his cast and crew, often pushing them into doing dangerous stunts, and there were numerous accidents during the filming.

Ironically, the first of these involved Hughes himself. A fledgling flyer, Hughes decided to try piloting one of the newly acquired planes, a Thomas Morse "Scout." Stunt pilot Frank Clarke warned him not to do it because the Scout had a rotary engine, and if it were banked in the same direction as the rotation, the aircraft might spin dangerously. Hughes, however, scoffed at the warning and proceeded to do a banked takeoff, got to about four hundred feet, then suddenly spun over and crashed. Everyone rushed to where the plane had come down and pulled Hughes from the wreckage. They were mostly concerned that he was alive and well because they did not want to lose their meal ticket!

In May 1928 during filming, pilot Al Wilson took off from Caddo Field, encountered fog as he approached the Hollywood area, and suddenly heard a snap. His propeller had spun off the plane! He quickly bailed out and landed on the roof of a house in Hollywood. The plane, luckily, crashed between two houses—both owned by people in the movie business—and no one on the ground was injured.

Other accidents, however, proved to be much more serious. Stunt pilot Al Johnson took off from Glendale Airport, hit some high-tension wires in the Griffith Park area, and fell into the bed of the Los Angeles River. The plane was engulfed in flames, and Johnson died several hours later in a Glendale hospital.

Hughes realized that dramatic cloud formations were important to getting good aerial footage, so at the end of the summer of 1928, he decided to move several planes to the Oakland, California, area, where he was assured there would be lots of clouds, in contrast to the clear Los Angeles skies. A pilot named Clement Phillips was flying one of the planes north but had to make an emergency landing before he got to Oakland. He did some repairs to the plane and took off, but the engine suddenly quit and he came down and crashed in a field. Phillips was killed instantly.

One of the final dramatic scenes in the film was the diving, spinning crash of a German "Gotha." A Sikorsky bomber had been repainted to simulate the plane, but most of the flyers involved in the film had refused to do the dangerous stunt. Al Wilson, however, agreed to take the plane up and bring it down in the risky dive. Since the plane was supposed to be on fire, a mechanical blower had been rigged in the Sikorsky to blast out black smoke. A young mechanic named Phil Jones volunteered to operate the smoke machine.

On March 22, 1929, with three camera planes recording the stunt, Wilson took the aircraft up to 7,500 feet. But as he started the dive, bits of fabric tore off the left wing and pieces of cowling from the engine broke away. Wilson, realizing he was in trouble, climbed out of the cockpit and pulled his ripcord. Jones, however, never got out and was killed when the plane hit the ground.

Wilson, shattered by the loss of Jones, swore he had yelled to the mechanic to jump, but it is likely he never heard him. An investigation into the accident exonerated Wilson, but he was so affected by the death that he gave up stunt flying. Sadly, Wilson himself would die in a plane crash in 1932.

Hell's Angels did not finish production until 1930. By this time, sound had been added to movies and audiences were shunning silent films, so Hughes decided to totally reshoot many of the scenes and record dialogue. The problem, however, was Greta Nissen's thick Norwegian accent, so she was replaced by a young, attractive platinum blonde named Jean Harlow. Harlow would eventually become a popular star, but one who would suffer a tragic series of events and an early death.

When the filming ended, Hughes, once again, decided to do most of the work himself, and quickly learned how to edit the thousands of feet he had shot and add the sound effects. Many of the sequences—especially those involving Harlow's awkward performance—proved to be rather amateurish, and even got laughs at some screenings. But the flying scenes brought the film to a technical level that thrilled audiences and would attract huge crowds.

The premiere was set for May 27, 1930, and Hughes was determined to make it the most lavish opening in movie history. Planes flew low over Hollywood Boulevard, dropping flares and parachutes. The street was blocked off on one side, but the eager crowds were immense, and all traffic came to a standstill. Although scheduled for an 8:15 start, the film did not begin until well after 10:00 p.m.

The initial screening was a huge success. On October 28, 1930, the film opened in London to a theater packed with royalty. Although the actors' poor British accents brought laughter, the audience was awed by the aerial scenes.

Ultimately, however, the $4 million budget, a huge sum for that era, was too much to recoup at a time when most theaters were charging 25 cents for a ticket, and Hughes had to admit that *Hell's Angels* would be a money loser. He had drained a vast amount of cash from his other enterprises, had shot almost three hundred times the amount of film that was eventually used, and had lavished many months' worth of his time and effort on the project.

In an interview some years later, Hughes admitted, "Making *Hell's Angels* by myself was my biggest mistake. . . . Trying to do the work of twelve men was just dumbness on my part. I learned by bitter experience that no one man can know everything."

MR. MAYER HAS A LITTLE MEETING

1927

He was, many believed, the most powerful man in Hollywood. He certainly commanded one of the biggest salaries. His name was Louis B. Mayer, and he boasted that his studio, Metro-Goldwyn-Mayer (MGM), had "more stars than there are in heaven."

In many ways, he was right.

Louis B. Mayer had come from Russia with his parents. By the age of twenty-three, he had taken over a rundown burlesque theater in Massachusetts, renovated it, and, in 1907, reopened it as a movie theater. Soon, along with a partner, he acquired more theaters, and in short order had the largest theater chain in New England.

In 1915 Mayer made a deal with D. W. Griffith for the exclusive rights to show *The Birth of a Nation* in New England (although he had not even seen the film), a deal that eventually earned him more than $100,000. The following year he moved to Los Angeles, and by 1924, through a series of mergers, he was instrumental in creating Metro-Goldwyn-Mayer, becoming the vice president in charge of production. For the next twenty-seven years, Louis B. Mayer almost single-handedly controlled each and every one of the numerous motion pictures made by MGM. In many ways, he also controlled many of the writers, directors, actors, and almost everyone else working in the movie industry.

But Mr. Mayer had a slight problem. In November 1926 nine Hollywood studios and five labor unions signed a contract called the Studio Basic Agreement. It had taken almost ten years to iron it out, but the agreement created contractual protection for the members of several craft unions who were employed in the motion picture business: stagehands, carpenters, electricians, painters, and musicians (who played mood music while silent films were being made). Mayer was well aware that it was only a matter of time before the actors, writers, and directors would also want to negotiate contracts, so he devised a clever ploy to circumvent this.

On New Year's Day 1927, he called together three important Hollywood players for a little dinner meeting: actor Conrad Nagel, who just happened to be under contract to Mayer's studio; Fred Niblo, who recently directed MGM's hit *Ben-Hur;* and Fred Beetson, who headed the Association of Motion Picture Producers. Mayer explained his idea of creating an organization to, he said, benefit all those in the motion picture business, although he may have been thinking of an organization to *control* those in the business. His guests liked the idea and spread the word to their associates. A week later, thirty-six members of the Hollywood community met at a second dinner and established the International Academy of Motion Picture Arts and Sciences ("International" was eventually dropped from the name).

Soon there were articles of incorporation, and in May 1927, 231 of Hollywood's elite met at a banquet at the Biltmore Hotel and became the first members of the organization. Buried in the list of the aims of the group was a line that stated that the Academy would

"encourage the improvement and advancement . . . of the profession
. . . by awards of merit for distinctive achievement."

Though probably no one at the time was aware of it, this brief
statement was the germ of an idea that would soon become the
Academy Awards. And these very awards would, in the years that followed, make and break many careers, cause disagreement and dissen-
sion, mean the difference between many films' success or failure, and
even provide lively wagers as to the result of the annual balloting.

It is interesting to note that at one of the early committee meet-
ings, designer Cedric Gibbons had sketched his idea for the award
statuette: a naked knight plunging a sword into a reel of film. Artist
George Stanley would soon model the image in clay (and receive
$500 for the job), and twelve copies of the bronze, gold-plated
images would become the first "Oscars." There is, however, some
disagreement over who coined the term "Oscar." Actress Bette Davis
claimed she did, but Academy librarian Margaret Herrick said she
had remarked that it reminded her of her uncle Oscar, and Hollywood columnist Sidney Skolsky also claimed he was the first to coin
the name in one of his columns.

In any event, in July 1928 the newly formed Academy announced
that awards would be given in twelve different areas: Production (the
"best" film of the year considering all elements); Artistic Quality of
Production (the most "artistic" or unique film of the year); Actor;
Actress; Director; Comedy Director (since many short comedies
were being made very profitably); Cinematography; Interior Deco-
ration; Engineering Effects; and writing awards for Adaptation,
Original Story, and Title Writing (most films were, at the time, still
silent). The balloting procedure was outlined by the Academy, and
the final tally (with some deliberations) was announced to the press
in February 1929. The actual presentation would not take place until
May 16, 1929, at a banquet at the Hollywood Roosevelt Hotel.

The first winner of the Academy Award for Production was the epic World War I film *Wings*. Interestingly, this would be the only silent film to win an Oscar, since sound erupted on the scene in the months that followed. The Artistic Quality winner was *Sunrise,* a gorgeously photographed tale of a farmer who, enticed by another woman, plans to murder his wife. This was the only year that this category existed, and the two "best picture" awards have been combined ever since. Unfortunately, in lists of Best Picture chosen by the Academy, *Sunrise* rarely even gets a mention.

The Best Director award was bestowed upon Frank Borzage for *Seventh Heaven.* Best Comedy Direction (this was the only year this award would be given) went to Lewis Milestone for *Two Arabian Knights.* Emil Jannings won Best Actor for his achievement in two films, *The Last Command* and *The Way of All Flesh.* Best Actress went to Janet Gaynor, who had appeared in *Seventh Heaven, Street Angel,* and *Sunrise.*

Two Special Awards were also given out that first year: Warner Brothers Studio received recognition for *The Jazz Singer,* "the pioneer talking picture, which has revolutionized the industry," and the Academy chose to finally recognize the neglected Charlie Chaplin "for versatility and genius in writing, acting, directing and producing *The Circus.*"

It was a gala evening, attended only by Academy members, who dined and danced, lauded each other, and gave out their awards. There was little reason, many felt, to make it a public event; it was a private party with a group of friends patting each other on the back. There were, however, many aspects of this first ceremony that would continue throughout the decades of Academy Awards that followed, though many things would also change. Most significant was the time lag between the announcement of the winners and the actual ceremony—a length of almost three months. The type and number of awards would also change over time, as would the importance of being a winner.

One thing that would persist, however, would be the speeches. Even though the winners did show some restraint, others, notably founder Louis B. Mayer, would expound eloquently about the Academy and its accomplishments and the major challenges in the years to come. That first evening ended with a song by Al Jolson.

The possible value of the awards was not overlooked by newspaper publisher William Randolph Hearst, who made certain that his columnist Louella Parsons would write in praise of the importance of the evening's events. No doubt Hearst had in mind promoting a future award for his mistress, actress Marion Davies.

The Academy had supposedly been created to promote the arts and sciences of motion picture production, but for Louis B. Mayer (as well as other producers), its creation had been an attempt to ward off the growing movement for actors, writers, and directors to organize. The Academy would, however, undergo numerous challenges to its existence over the ensuing years, and even the possibility of complete collapse.

That first ceremony had all the glitz and glamour one would expect from Hollywood, but there were many problems ahead for the fledgling organization—an organization that had its beginnings on that New Year's Day in 1927 when Mr. Mayer had a little meeting.

THE MOUSE THAT ROARED

1928

The two couples had enjoyed their leisurely lunch, and now with their wives off shopping, the men sat down in the modest New York office to discuss business. Behind the desk Charles Mintz smiled as he began to outline plans for distribution of the films the other man would be producing.

The other man was Walter Elias Disney, whose series of cartoons with a character named Oswald the Lucky Rabbit were becoming quite popular with audiences. Disney felt confident he could increase the requested fee for each future film and that Mintz would have no qualms about agreeing.

Instead, what he heard from the other man hit him like a bombshell.

Mintz made his offer: He was cutting the advance for each cartoon from $2,250 to $1,800. If Disney disagreed, Mintz would take over production with his own company, and he would even hire Disney's artists. He carefully explained that the character of Oswald was owned and controlled by him. There would be no negotiation.

Disney left the office shattered. A call to his brother Roy in Los Angeles confirmed the fact that Mintz owned the character of Oswald. Roy also provided the additional bad news that four of their top animators had already resigned and gone over to Mintz's company.

On the long train ride back across the country, Walt explained the situation to his wife, Lillian. Somewhere on that cross-country ride, Disney came up with an idea. He needed a new cartoon character—what about a cute little mouse?

When he got back to his studio in California, he showed a rough sketch to fellow artist Ub Iwerks. There are many who believe that Iwerks was the most creative of the Disney artists, the true staff genius, and even that Disney got the credit while Iwerks did the work.

Iwerks made some changes in Disney's sketch, producing the first images of a cute little mouse. Disney liked what he saw and at first wanted to call him Mortimer, but his wife disagreed. Mortimer, she felt, was too highfalutin a name for a cartoon mouse. "Call him Mickey," she suggested, and Mickey it would be. But even though the little mouse had now come to life, he still had a long way to go. And so did his creator, Walt Disney.

Walter Elias Disney was born in Chicago on December 5, 1901. His father, Elias Disney, experienced a number of financial setbacks and eventually took the family (now with five children) to Kansas City, Missouri. After a brief stint in the ambulance corps in World War I, young Walt got a job with a local art studio, where he met Ubbe ("Ub") Iwerks, a man who would have a major influence on Disney's life. Soon Walt and Ub set up their own business and later got jobs with the Kansas City Film Ad Company making simple animated commercials for local theaters.

The year was 1919, and the art of animation in films was in its infancy. Winsor McCay, who had created the comic-strip character Little Nemo, had put him in a film, and McCay had also produced a short film called *Gertie the Dinosaur*. For Gertie, McCay had drawn sketches for each movement, repeating the background on each sketch. This caused the surroundings to jiggle as Gertie moved, since they could not be kept in perfect alignment. The solution to this problem—transparent cels—would not be invented until later, when an artist named Earl Hurd came up with the idea of drawing the characters on transparent sheets of celluloid and photographing them with a single background to avoid the jumping effect. Ultimately, this would become the standard for animators for many years to come.

Disney, just eighteen years old, borrowed a movie camera and experimented with some short animated films he called "Laugh-O-Grams," which he then sold to a local movie theater. Now confident of his skill, he left the Kansas City Film Ad Company and started creating animated movies on his own. He began by making short films based on updated fairy tales, and then in 1923 decided to make a film incorporating a human character (a young girl named Virginia Davis) with some animated characters. He called it *Alice's Wonderland.*

With finances tight, however, Walt felt it was time to move his operation, and chose to go west to Los Angeles, where his brother Roy was in the veterans' hospital recovering from tuberculosis. Setting up a small animation studio in a garage, he was able to negotiate a contract with New York distributor Margaret Winkler to supply one "Alice" picture a month. He hired more people, including his old friend Ub Iwerks and a young lady named Lillian Bounds. A romance soon blossomed, and in July 1925 Walt and Lillian were married.

After sixty episodes of *Alice's Wonderland,* it was time for a new character, and this was when Iwerks came up with Oswald the Lucky Rabbit. The series of films they did with the Oswald character proved to be a success, but the distributor, Margaret Winkler, had married a man named Charles Mintz, and it was Disney's confrontation with

Mintz that provided the impetus that resulted in the lucky creation of Mickey Mouse.

In addition to Iwerks's graphic skill and Walt's ideas, there was another significant factor that would contribute to Mickey's success. In October 1927, *The Jazz Singer* introduced sound to the motion picture screen, and it became a huge success. Disney quickly realized that this was the direction movies were going, and it was the direction he would take his animated mouse.

His artists had already begun working on two silent Mickey cartoons, *Plane Crazy* and *The Gallopin' Gaucho,* but Disney set them aside and decided to produce a Mickey film that would be designed with a sound track in mind. With a metronome to keep the beat, one of his animators playing the harmonica, and Walt and other artists doing sound effects with cowbells and tin plates, they projected a sequence from their new film for their wives. The film was silent, but the men provided music and effects to the beat of the metronome. The experiment worked, and they began to realize how a sound track could be used with animated films.

The film was ultimately called *Steamboat Willie,* and after Disney had a musical score created for it (though it took several tries), the short cartoon opened at the Colony Theater in New York on November 18, 1928. Cleverly, a promoter named Harry Reichenbach, who had already seen the cartoon and made the deal with Walt to show it as a sneak preview, had contacted all his friends in the press to let them know that something special would be taking place that day.

The reviews came out the next day, and they were ecstatic, with both *Variety* and the *New York Times* lauding Disney's achievement. The little mouse was on his way. With a deal made for distribution of the Mickey Mouse cartoons, over the next year and a half Walt's studio produced thirty-one shorts starring Mickey. His popularity soared, and soon he became better known and even more popular than real-life movie stars like Al Jolson, Buster Keaton, and even Charlie Chaplin.

The Mickey that appeared in the first cartoons was, in many ways, much different from the respectful, well-behaved mouse we know today. He was very mischievous and, in some scenes, even cruel. Walt himself provided the original voice for Mickey, and he would do so for about twenty years. Mickey's appearance changed as well. Soon he had gloves and shoes, and eventually his personality would become much more lovable.

The production of the sound films also improved. Gradually they evolved the process of recording the voices first so the animators could work to match the existing sound track. Disney hired an old Kansas City friend, musician Carl Stalling, who had been an accompanist on silent films, to work on the music for the cartoons.

However, in 1930 two crucial members of Walt's staff left the studio. Ub Iwerks was wooed away, and Carl Stalling also left. But Disney pushed on, buoyed by the continuing popularity of Mickey; his other series, the *Silly Symphonies*; and his acquisition of several new artists. With a staff now numbering more than forty people, in 1932, despite the additional cost, he decided to make one of the *Silly Symphonies* in color. It was called "Flowers and Trees" and utilized the Technicolor process. Disney signed a deal with the Technicolor Company for exclusive animation rights to their process for the next two years.

Mickey Mouse continued to build a worldwide reputation, and the Mickey films (still being made in black and white) could be seen everywhere. In Italy he was called Topolino, and in Japan, Miki Kuchi. *Time* magazine even devoted a feature article to the mouse in 1931. In the years that followed, merchandisers made deals with the Disney organization, and Mickey items were being sold around the world. By 1935 it was estimated that Disney-licensed items would generate over $35 million in sales. Most notable was the ubiquitous Mickey Mouse watch, made by the Ingersoll watch company and sold by the millions.

Over the years that followed, Mickey Mouse would become known to children and adults everywhere, as he appeared in films, the Disney theme parks, and many items of merchandise. The little mouse created in 1928 had not only carved a spot in history, but was in many ways responsible for saving Disney's studio and establishing Walt Disney as a preeminent figure in motion picture history.

THE ACTRESS AND
THE HOLLYWOOD SIGN

1932

To many people, it is the symbol of Hollywood. To others, it's just an eyesore.

Visitors and locals alike make pilgrimages and climb Mount Lee to get close, though most folks just casually glance at it from below. It has appeared in several movies, many of which have parodied and made fun of it. Yet it has stood for more than eighty years and will probably remain for many more. It is that huge edifice that looks down at Hollywood that is simply called "the Hollywood Sign." And it has a history all its own.

Real estate has always been a prime mover in Southern California, and many people have made large fortunes buying and selling property. In 1923 two developers named Woodruff and Shoults were selling lots on the south side of the Hollywood Hills and had named the 500-acre development "Hollywoodland." H. J. Whitley, who was also developing property, suggested to his friend Harry Chandler, who was at the time owner of the *Los Angeles Times* and also a partner in the Hollywoodland syndicate, that a big sign might prove success-ful in attracting buyers.

The Crescent Sign Company was hired to do the job, and Thomas Goff, owner of the company, designed a sign with thirteen letters, each thirty feet wide and fifty feet high. Made of wood and sheet metal, each of the letters was studded with more than four thousand light-bulbs. On July 13, 1923, the sign was officially dedicated. It was never intended to last more than a year or two, since the developers felt the lots would all be sold by then. However, as the popularity of movies grew over the years and as the term "Hollywood" became closely asso-ciated with the industry, the sign soon became a landmark.

Unfortunately, the life and death of one actress was to become intimately involved with the Hollywood Sign. Her name was Peg Entwistle.

Born in London, England, in 1908, Lillian Millicent Entwistle was brought to New York City while still a child by her father after her mother's death. Tragically, her father was killed in a traffic accident, and Peg, now a teenager, decided to pursue a career as an actress. At seventeen she first appeared in a play with a Boston reper-tory company, and soon was getting small roles in Broadway plays. At the age of nineteen she married actor Robert Keith, unaware that he had been married before and had a six-year-old son. (Interestingly, the child, named Brian, would grow up to become the noted actor Brian Keith.) The marriage, however, would shortly end in divorce.

Peg Entwistle had several stage successes, appearing with Doro-thy Gish in *Getting Married* and with Laurette Taylor in *Alice Sit-By-The-Fire*. But it was the early thirties, and the country was feeling the effects of the Great Depression. The theater scene in New York had been reduced to a trickle, and there was little work there for actors. Peg Entwistle decided to go west, since the movies still seemed to be providing opportunities for acting work.

In April 1932 Peg arrived in Los Angeles with great aspirations, but little money. After a stay at the Hollywood Studio Club (a women's residence hotel), she decided to save money by moving in with her Uncle Harold, who had a modest little house on Beachwood Canyon Drive. She got some stage work in a play called *The Mad Hopes* with popular actress Billie Burke, but the show only had a brief run. She was then signed by RKO for a part in a murder-mystery film called *Thirteen Women,* which starred Irene Dunne, but the critical reviews were poor and the studio did not release it. Even worse, RKO did not renew the option on her contract.

Despondent, Peg decided her only choice was to go back to New York, where she at least had had some success, but she was unable to raise the money for the train fare. On September 18, 1932, the severely depressed twenty-four-year-old actress climbed the road that led up to the huge Hollywoodland sign. Leaving her coat and purse on the ground, she climbed the ladder used by electricians to replace burned out lightbulbs, and fifty feet up, leapt to her death from the giant *H.*

Her suicide made headlines, but the identity of the woman who had been found was initially unknown. It was not until her uncle saw the newspaper and realized she had not come back to the house that the full effect of what had happened hit him. He went to the morgue and identified her body.

Ironically, a letter arrived several days later at her uncle's house from the Beverly Hills Playhouse. It had been mailed the day before Peg's death. The letter offered her a lead role in their next play—the story of a young woman who commits suicide.

The tragedy of Peg Entwistle was, in a way, a foreshadowing of the gradual deterioration of the sign itself. Over the years that followed, bits of the letters began to fall, and the letter *A* was knocked over by a car driven by Albert Kothe, who, even though he had been appointed caretaker of the sign, had been driving up the mountain while slightly inebriated.

In 1949 the Hollywood Chamber of Commerce signed a contract with the City of Los Angeles Parks Department accepting responsibility to maintain the sign and to remove the last four letters so that it said merely "Hollywood," making it a more appropriate landmark. Funds were limited, however, and the sign continued to fall apart.

Finally, in 1978 a concerted effort, spurred by rock performer Alice Cooper, was made to raise the money needed for a new sign. With nine donors—including cowboy star Gene Autry, singer Andy Williams, and *Playboy* publisher Hugh Hefner, as well as Cooper—$250,000 was raised, and the new sign was unveiled on November 14, 1978, Hollywood's seventy-fifth anniversary. The new letters were made of steel, and they were most recently repainted in 2005. The sign is now protected by a security system with motion detectors and closed-circuit cameras. Movement closer than fifty yards from the letters sets off an alarm.

Although it is illegal to make any alterations to the sign, numerous interesting changes have been made over the years by blocking off parts of letters, often done surreptitiously at night. In 1987 when Pope John Paul II visited Los Angeles, the sign became HOLY-WOOD. In 1992 when Ross Perot entered the presidential race, it became PEROTWOOD. In 1993 twenty members of a UCLA fraternity changed it to GO UCLA before the annual USC-UCLA football game. The fraternity members, however, were charged with trespassing, and it was this incident that led to the installation of the security system. On January 1, 2000, flashing lights illuminated the sign in celebration of the new millennium.

Currently the sign is protected and promoted by the Hollywood Sign Trust, a nonprofit organization. The trust has the responsibility of maintaining and repairing the sign, as well as raising money to educate the world about the sign's historical and cultural importance.

You can see the sign from many vantage points in Hollywood, and it constantly keeps everyone aware of this one-of-a-kind place in the heart of Los Angeles. The history of the sign, with its tragedy, its silliness, and its blatant commercialism, seems to fit perfectly with this place called Hollywood—a place known for the many images it creates in the minds of people the world over.

THE MONKEY ON THE ROOF

1933

Millions of Americans were suffering through the Great Depression. Unemployment was rampant, and times were tough everywhere. Yet on March 2, 1933, a motion picture opened simultaneously at two of New York's biggest theaters: Radio City Music Hall and the New Roxy. Crowds flocked to both movie houses to see a stage show and a film that was to be talked about for years to come.

In its first four days the film brought in almost $90,000, a new all-time attendance record for any indoor attraction in the world. And even with ten shows daily, seats remained at a premium and the theaters could barely keep up with public demand. *King Kong* had landed in New York.

What was the reason for the amazing popularity of a movie about a fifty-foot ape that terrorizes New York? Why was the public so eager to see lovely Fay Wray in the clutches of this huge monster? And perhaps most curious of all, how had this bizarre concept for a film ever come to be in the first place?

Three individuals were predominantly responsible for *King Kong:* Merian C. Cooper, Ernest B. Schoedsack, and Willis H. O'Brien. Many others were involved, but it was these three men who made this absolutely crazy concept come to life. Cooper and Schoedsack had met while serving in World War I, and after the armistice they got together to make some classic documentary films in faraway places. These included *Grass* in 1925, following a tribe on the shores of the Persian Gulf; *Chang* in 1927 in northern Siam (Thailand); and *Rango* in 1931, a story that partly takes place in the jungles of India.

It was Cooper who originally came up with the idea of a giant ape, and in 1931 he was hired by his friend David O. Selznick, who had been put in charge of production at RKO Studios. Cooper was impressed by the animation photography of Willis O'Brien, who was working at RKO on a special-effects film called *Creation.* O'Brien was a highly skilled technician and an expert at making small animal models move by stop-frame animation. In this technique the models are moved a fraction of an inch, then one or two frames of film are exposed, then the models are moved another fraction and again photographed. By this slow and intensive procedure, inanimate models of creatures would seem to come to life when the developed film was projected.

O'Brien agreed to work with Cooper (*Creation* was never completed) on his ape idea, and they prepared a sample reel in which a model of the ape battles a prehistoric creature, as well as some other scenes with the miniature monkey. The folks at RKO were impressed and agreed to invest money in a feature film that employed O'Brien's special effects. Cooper got his partner, Ernest Schoedsack, to help with producing and directing the film, and once a script was ready, production began in May 1932.

A host of special effects were employed, including stop-frame animation, rear projections of images on a screen behind the actors, and even "glass shots" in which a glass slide is put in front of the camera lens to add foreground material (like vegetation) to the scene. Despite some criticism of the script, Cooper and Schoedsack insisted that the entrance of the huge ape be delayed until almost an hour into the film.

Soundman Murray Spivak added the roars of Kong by recording lions and tigers at the zoo, then slowing down the tape and rerecording the sounds. He also devised numerous other clever ways to produce the sound effects in the movie. Talented composer Max Steiner had been hired by RKO in 1929 to orchestrate music for several films, and when music was needed in just four weeks for the western spectacle *Cimarron,* he came up with an excellent score. For *King Kong,* Steiner timed each scene with a stopwatch, created themes for different sections, and then conducted an eighty-piece orchestra for the recording session.

Primed by lots of advance publicity and word of mouth, audiences quickly made the film a must-see experience. And this is what they saw: Film director Carl Denham (played by Robert Armstrong) has chartered a ship to take him to a mysterious island. He convinces a young lady named Ann Darrow (Fay Wray) to come along for the adventure (she also happens to be hungry and out of work). But when they finally reach the uncharted island, Ann is captured by the local natives. Denham and the crew go ashore and soon discover she is being offered as the "bride of Kong." It is then that we see for the first time the huge ape that soon takes Ann to his lair. Now they must rescue her.

After many harrowing adventures, Denham and his crew, with the heroism of first mate John Driscoll (Bruce Cabot), save Ann and also subdue the huge Kong with gas grenades. Denham decides to bring Kong back to civilization by building a raft and towing him back to New York City, though we don't see exactly how this is accomplished. Kong is chained on a Broadway stage for exhibit to the public, but he breaks free, grabs Ann through the window of a hotel room, and, wreaking fear and devastation as he moves through the city, finally climbs the Empire State Building. Airplanes are summoned to stop him, and they fire at him atop the building. He is mortally wounded, but carefully puts down the screaming Ann before he falls to his death on the street below.

The film was, in essence, a basic story of beauty and the beast with a strong erotic subtext, and many in the audience, while they enjoyed the thrill of it all, may also have seen Kong as a symbol of the Depression, wreaking havoc on the city but finally subdued. But it was also the most marvelous of escapist films, and just the thing audiences needed to take their minds off the hard times they were living in.

Reviews were generally positive, but they mostly showed great admiration for the special effects. While these effects may appear primitive by the standards of today's computer graphic wizardry, in 1933 they amazed audiences, and to a large extent they still remain amazing to spectators today.

According to the producer, Merian Cooper, the actual cost of making *King Kong* was $430,000, but the studio tacked on various overhead costs, and the figure they reported as the "official" production cost of the film was $650,000.

The box office returns, however, were huge, and were enough to pull RKO out of debt for the first time.

The film was rereleased in 1938, with some scenes edited out, and again did excellent business. It seems that the Hays Office (the office created to oversee film content) was unhappy with the sequences of Kong's vicious attack on the native village, Kong biting a pedestrian to death in the New York rampage scene, and Kong dropping a woman to her death as he searches for Ann. The most talked-about scene that was cut was when Kong (in the jungle) peels off Ann's dress and sniffs his finger.

King Kong was released twice more, in 1942 and 1952, and generated more profits. (Today it is easily available on DVD since the copyright has long since expired.) A sequel was quickly released in 1933 called *Son of Kong* to capitalize on the success of the original, but it was more comic than scary. In 1949 another ape film, *Mighty Joe Young,* was released, directed by Ernest Schoedsack and with Willis O'Brien again supplying special effects.

The Kong story has been twice remade and updated for modern audiences. The 1976 version (the film debut of Jessica Lange in the Fay Wray role) was not well received. However, the 2005 *King Kong,* directed by Peter Jackson (who had recently successfully made *Lord of the Rings*), kept more to the original and attracted a large and eager audience.

What the 1933 film did, however, was inspire an entirely new interest in the possibilities of film special effects, as well as generate a host of monster movies that would follow over the years. In spite of the sequels, copies, and remakes, it is generally acknowledged that the original *King Kong* was the film that broke new ground and would take its place as a milestone in cinema history.

FRANK SAVES OSCAR

1936

The situation was close to desperate. Though it had initially been formed to, supposedly, advance the arts and sciences of the motion picture industry, in 1936 the Academy of Motion Picture Arts and Sciences (AMPAS) was in shambles.

It all stemmed from labor relations and the simple fact that as an organization that in many ways was controlled by the studios, AMPAS was not in a position to bargain for the writers, actors, and directors. These three groups had created their own "guilds," and they were quickly moving away from any domination by the Academy. In fact, the guilds had become so disillusioned by the behavior of the Academy that many actors, writers, and directors had withdrawn their membership.

The Screen Actors Guild, led by Ronald Reagan (the very same Ronald Reagan who would become president of the United States); the Writers Guild, led by John Howard Lawson (who would become one of the blacklisted Hollywood Ten); and the newly formed Directors Guild, led by King Vidor, were urging their members to leave the Academy and to boycott the upcoming awards banquet. The leadership of the guilds saw the Academy as a "company organization," inimical to the needs of those who worked in films.

As the date approached for the eighth awards event, many directors were planning not to attend, and telegrams had gone out to members of the actors and writers guilds urging them not to attend and not to accept any Oscars. Membership in the Academy had plummeted from six hundred to a mere forty. Financially, the organization was in dire straits.

The man who had recently been chosen as president of this foundering organization was Frank Capra. His industry reputation was a solid one, having the previous year made a virtual sweep of awards with his charming film *It Happened One Night,* winning Best Picture, Best Director, Best Actor (Clark Gable), and Best Actress (Claudette Colbert).

Born in Italy in 1897, Capra had come with his parents to the United States at the age of six. After attending college at what is now the California Institute of Technology in 1918, he enlisted in the U.S. Army. After his service, he became interested in the film business and got a job as a prop man for silent comedies. Soon he was writing gags for the films, and eventually advanced to directing. His big break came when Columbia Pictures' head Harry Cohn hired him to write, direct, and even co-produce films. His *Lady for a Day* won him an Academy Award nomination, but no win. *It Happened One Night,* however, would bring him overwhelming success, both at the Academy Awards and at the box office.

As president of the Academy, Capra was now confronted with a collapsing organization, and an awards ceremony with almost no one choosing to attend. But he had a brilliant idea: Why not make the awards ceremony a tribute to a man who had done so much for the film business, but who had, in many ways, been slighted over the years and virtually forgotten? At the age of sixty-one, David Wark Griffith had just married his fourth wife, and though his career had long been in decline, was definitely a movie icon. The evening would be a tribute to the grand old man who had made cinema history with *The Birth of a Nation* and *Intolerance.*

Griffith agreed to attend, and he received a standing ovation as he entered the room. His presence had helped to expand the number of attendees at the event, but only twenty members of the Actors Guild and thirteen of the Writers Guild made an appearance. Fortunately, two major winners were present to receive their statuettes: Victor McLaglen, who won Best Actor for his role in the Irish Rebellion drama *The Informer,* and Bette Davis, who won Best Actress for her wildly dramatic turn in *Dangerous.*

The winning film was MGM's *Mutiny on the Bounty,* based on the true story (popularized in a novel written by Charles Nordhoff and James Norman Hall) of a sailors' mutiny on a ship commanded by a tyrannical captain, played with delicious venom by Charles Laughton. MGM's head of production, Irving Thalberg, was, fortunately, on hand to receive the award. However, two other major winners—Dudley Nichols, writer of *The Informer* script, and John Ford, director of the film—chose not to make an appearance.

After the awards banquet, Capra found himself in an awkward situation when the Academy sent the Oscar to Nichols's home. The writer returned it with a note saying that acceptance of the award would mean turning his back on members of his guild, who had ventured everything in their struggle for a "genuine writers' organization." Capra tried sending it a second time, saying that the competition does not take into account "the personal or economic views of the nominees," but his attempt was in vain, and Nichols again sent the Oscar back.

It was a different story, however, in the case of John Ford, who was treasurer of the Directors Guild: He agreed to accept the award. In a small ceremony, Capra presented the Oscar to Ford, but in reprisal, Ford was voted out of office by his own guild.

Frank Capra had succeeded in pulling off the awards ceremony and keeping the Academy functioning, but there was still more to be done. He worked to change the rules for nominations, creating a special Awards Nominating Committee appointed by the president and made up of fifty members from each of the five branches. The final vote, as before, would be made by the entire Academy membership.

Capra also worked hard to get the Academy out of the political arena and to concentrate its efforts on education and promotion of motion pictures. This would be a significant step toward making the Motion Picture Academy an impartial organization and not one dominated by the studio bosses.

After serving four years as Academy president, Capra was elected president of the Directors Guild, and he would direct some motion picture classics in the years that followed. Since many of the films he made were sentimental stories that pitted ordinary people against business or government, his work was often called "Capra-corn." His movies were, however, popular with the public—especially during the years Americans suffered from the tribulations of the Great Depression.

Among his most popular films were *Mr. Deeds Goes to Town* (1936), the story of a man who inherits $20 million and wants to give it away to the needy; *You Can't Take It With You* (1938), about a strange and wacky family; *Mr. Smith Goes to Washington* (1939), the story of an idealist who goes to Washington and encounters nothing but corruption; and the perennial Christmas classic about a man who wants to end his life and is saved by a bumbling angel named Clarence, *It's a Wonderful Life* (1946). His World War II documentary films were an important contribution to the war effort, and his series of films called *Why We Fight* were shown to American servicemen to explain the rise and dangers of the Nazi and Japanese threat.

Frank Capra died in 1991 at the age of ninety-four. He left a legacy of many outstanding films, many of which continue to charm audiences even today. And he was a major contributor to making the Academy of Motion Picture Arts and Sciences the important international organization it remains.

DESPERATELY SEEKING A SCARLETT

1937–1938

No one was very interested. Irving Thalberg at MGM told his boss, Louis B. Mayer, that Civil War pictures just didn't make money. (He may have forgotten that Mayer had gotten started in the film business exhibiting something called *The Birth of a Nation.*) Jack Warner at Warner Brothers turned it down, and Universal was not interested in doing a "costume" picture. Pandro Berman, a producer at RKO, felt it would cost too much to make. Finally, David O. Selznick made an offer of $50,000, and the offer was accepted.

What was this property that just about everybody in Hollywood had turned down? It was a sprawling novel about the Civil War and Reconstruction, and it had, at various times, been given the titles *Bugles Sang True, Tote the Weary Load,* and *Tomorrow Is Another Day.* The book that seemed to have no possibility of becoming a film had been written by a young woman from Atlanta, Georgia, whom most people knew as Peggy Marsh. The fact that the publisher, Macmillan, was about to release the book was also due to a series of accidents. Marsh had almost changed her mind about having a publisher even read it, but it was read, and the publisher liked it.

Now using her married name, Margaret Mitchell, her saga of the Civil War, at this point called *Gone With the Wind,* was about to appear in print. She would receive an advance against royalties of just $250. The advance, however, was only a small down payment. From the moment it appeared, the book took off and copies raced off the shelves, bought by excited readers.

The clever Mr. Selznick was now sitting pretty with a property that an eager public would want to see. Just thirty-six years old in 1938, he had come from a movie family. His father, Lewis Selznick, had been a successful distributor of silent films (though he went broke in 1923), and with his connections, David got a job at MGM, then at Paramount Pictures. He then moved to RKO as head of production and was responsible for a number of profitable films—including the 1933 blockbuster *King Kong.* But Selznick wanted his own studio, and in 1935 he accomplished just that. Selznick International Pictures became a reality, and for the next few years produced several successful motion pictures.

And now he owned the film rights to *Gone With the Wind.*

With readers all over the country devouring Mitchell's book, speculation ran wild as to who would play the two critical roles of Rhett Butler and Scarlett O'Hara. In Hollywood as well, major actors and actresses knew that these two parts promised to be the most talked about for years to come, making them roles that were coveted by virtually every film performer.

The choice of debonair Clark Gable to play Rhett Butler seemed an easy one, but in those days movie stars were contracted to individual studios, and MGM controlled Gable's career. Interestingly, Selznick had not only worked at MGM, he had also married Louis Mayer's daughter Irene, but Mayer was not going to give up Gable easily. When negotiations were finally concluded, Selznick got Gable but had to give MGM the rights to distribute the film and 50 percent of the profits for the first few years.

But who would play the role of the headstrong, vivacious Southern belle whose story formed much of the strength of the book? The first to be screen-tested was Tallulah Bankhead, but she was in her thirties and at the start of the book Scarlett is in her teens. Norma Shearer, the widow of MGM's Irving Thalberg (he had tragically died in 1936), was eager for the part, but she was thirty-seven and, Selznick felt, also too mature to play the young Scarlett.

Selznick decided to launch a nationwide talent search for an unknown actress, someone audiences would not identify with other roles. Whether or not he really intended to find his Scarlett this way is open to speculation, though he had successfully done this to cast the child leads in his productions of *David Copperfield* and *Tom Sawyer*. But if nothing else, it guaranteed a huge amount of publicity for the movie, and once the word was out, letters and telephone calls began pouring into his studio. From all over the country—and from Europe as well—women sent their pictures and letters explaining why they would be the perfect Scarlett.

Selznick then sent his representatives to various parts of the country to do interviews. The appearance of these talent scouts made front-page stories in newspapers, and the articles often got more space than more important national and international news. George Cukor, who had been chosen to direct the film, was sent to the South, and he interviewed hundreds of Southern beauties who had some community theater or college acting experience. A few were even chosen to be sent to New York for screen tests.

Back in Hollywood, young women arrived at Selznick's studio in buses and cabs and on foot, all wanting to be tested. Actresses would try almost anything to get the part. On Christmas Day in 1937, a huge box shaped like a book—with an enlarged cover of Mitchell's novel on it—arrived at Selznick's home. Suddenly it opened, and there was a young lady dressed in period costume, proclaiming that she was Scarlett O'Hara!

But once the deal had been made with Clark Gable (who had initially resisted taking the part), and a start date had been set for February 1939, Selznick knew that the pressure to cast a Scarlett was on him. His brother Myron ran a talent agency, and he was enjoying the fruits of the Scarlett search by signing up many of the talented actresses who were after the part and were referred to him by brother David. One of Myron's clients was twenty-four-year-old Paulette Goddard, who had recently appeared in Charlie Chaplin's *Modern Times* and had, she said, married Chaplin as well (he was fifty at the time and had been married twice before).

David felt she might be just right for the part, put her under contract to his studio, and had her coached in acquiring a Southern accent. He even did some elaborate screen tests with Goddard that were directed by George Cukor. But when word got out that she was possibly the top contender for the part, there was a hue and cry from the public. It seems that she could not prove she and Chaplin were legally married, and letters poured in threatening boycotts of the film if she were chosen. So, fearing it might cost him dearly at the box office, especially with the huge investment the film would take, Selznick withdrew Goddard from consideration.

Atlanta was burning, or at least it was burning on the back lot of Selznick's studio. Pressured by investors to get the film started, Selznick had his art department build facades in front of some old sets that were gathering dust on the lot, and had his special effects man rig a way to control a fire. The local fire department was on hand, just in case, and lots of spectators had been told to show up to witness the dramatic conflagration.

Technicolor cameras were set up all over to get the shots, and doubles for Rhett and Scarlett were ready to drive their wagon through the flaming buildings. Selznick sat up on a platform, controlling the strength of the blaze with all the fervor of a kid with a monumental toy. As the inferno roared and the cameras rolled, Selznick was suddenly aware of brother Myron standing near him with a young lady in tow.

Myron turned to him and smiled as he pointed to the young lady. "I want you to meet Scarlett O'Hara," he said. Selznick would later recall that looking at the striking young woman with the light of the fires burning behind her, he was immediately taken with her appearance and could clearly visualize her in the part of Scarlett. The young lady was a British actress named Vivien Leigh.

But Selznick was still not certain, and had Leigh screen-tested as one of the four finalists for the part. The others were Jean Arthur, Joan Bennett, and Paulette Goddard. (Selznick was still considering Goddard despite his previous fears that choosing her might damage the box office returns.) Director George Cukor quickly saw the verve and passion in Leigh's interpretation of the part, and felt that they had finally found their Scarlett. After looking at all the tests, Selznick agreed.

At a Christmas party in 1938, Vivien Leigh arrived with actor Laurence Olivier. Cukor took her aside and said the part of Scarlett had been cast. Leigh accepted the statement with resignation, assuming it was one of the others. When she asked who had been chosen, Cukor smiled: "I guess we're stuck with you."

CITIZEN HEARST VS. *CITIZEN KANE*

1941

Everyone seemed to agree that Orson Welles was a genius. Just twenty-five years old, he had already made his mark as an actor, director, and writer, as well as scaring a good percentage of the U.S. population by directing and narrating a radio program based on the science-fiction novel *The War of the Worlds* that made many believe that Earth was being invaded by aliens.

In 1941 he had been invited to come to Hollywood by RKO Pictures president George Schaefer to make two films. After much deliberation, Welles came up with the idea of a story about a newspaper publisher and his rise to prominence, but the publisher is a man whose personal life and relationships are in shambles. He hired skilled writer Herman J. Mankiewicz to develop the script, but then realized that he was developing it as a straightforward narrative. So Welles restructured the script, making it a story told in flashbacks.

Orson Welles had virtually been given complete control over his project—including script, cast, crew, and final cut—and the result was *Citizen Kane.* He had co-written it, he had directed it, and he had starred in it. And, in many ways, it is an amazing motion picture.

Loosely based on the life of publisher William Randolph Hearst, the film broke new ground in style and technique. The story is told in a series of flashbacks as a reporter, after the publisher named John Foster Kane has died, seeks to uncover details of Kane's life by interviewing his former wives, associates, and others who knew him. The film, however, does not tell the story in a straightforward, linear way, but jumps around as the reporter tries to assemble the jigsaw puzzle and discover who the real Kane was and the truth about his life.

Having spent much of the first months he was in Hollywood intensively watching dozens of films, Welles learned a great deal about what could be done in a movie. This led him to use a variety of unusual cinematic techniques: a mock newsreel depicting the publisher's life; eerie photography of characters in silhouette; quick cuts in time and style; jarring moments that surprise the viewer as to location; long takes where characters talk without any cuts; sound that comes in from another scene before the first one has finished; and numerous other surprising—and refreshing—effects.

The problem was that William Randolph Hearst was still very much alive. The film was quite the unflattering portrait, and Hearst had many powerful friends in Hollywood (not to mention that his mistress was film star Marion Davies). When gossip columnist Hedda Hopper saw an advance screening of the movie, she was appalled at the way Hearst was depicted. And when rival columnist Louella Parsons, who wrote for Hearst newspapers, found out about the movie, she demanded a screening and arrived accompanied by two of Hearst's lawyers.

After seeing *Citizen Kane,* Parsons demanded that RKO's president, George Schaefer, shelve the picture, and warned the management of Radio City Music Hall, where it was soon due to open, that they should not show it. She had apparently talked to Hearst, and he had threatened to use his papers to expose the private lives of important Hollywood people, since the film supposedly showed his secret life. Welles himself was vulnerable, since at the time he was having an affair with the beautiful actress Dolores Del Rio.

Worse yet, Hearst was threatening to block the release of the film altogether. There was also a rumor (never officially proved) that movie mogul Louis B. Mayer, a friend of Hearst's, had offered RKO a huge sum to buy the film so he could have it destroyed.

With Hearst's lawyers threatening to bring a libel suit against both RKO and Welles, the director threatened to sue RKO for breach of contract if they gave in to pressure and pulled the movie. Welles even announced that he would buy the film from RKO for a million dollars (though it was doubtful he had that kind of money).

The studio finally agreed to open the film in May 1941, but Radio City Music Hall still refused to run it, so it was scheduled for the Palace Theater. There had already been some advance reviews, and they were extremely positive. *Newsweek* called Welles "the best actor in the history of acting," and reviewer John O'Hara said the film was the best picture he had ever seen. *Time* magazine wrote, "It has found important new techniques in picture-making and story-telling," while *Life* proclaimed, "Few movies have ever come from Hollywood with such powerful narrative, such original technique, such exciting photography."

Yet the many newspapers run by Hearst refused to run ads for *Citizen Kane* and, though the publisher never did bring a libel lawsuit, many distributors did not want to handle the film for fear Hearst might sue them after the movie was running. Hearst had also intimidated some of the theater chains by threatening to ban advertising of all their other films if they showed Welles's picture.

Despite the substantial publicity, however, the public did not flock to the theaters to see what all the fuss was about. Instead, they were, as Welles himself later said, "too scared of it to know what it even was." The box office receipts were dismal, and the film barely made its cost back. At the Academy Awards ceremony the following year, *Citizen Kane* got nine nominations but won only for Best Original Screenplay.

RKO eventually shelved the film, but it was rereleased in 1956. It now attracted the attention of a whole new audience, first new French directors such as Francois Truffaut and Jean-Luc Godard, and later the hundreds of students who studied it as a primer of inventive film technique.

Over the years the stature of *Citizen Kane* has grown immeasurably, and it continues to be listed by scholars and critics as one of the greatest American films of all time. In 1998 the American Film Institute surveyed a large number of film-industry professionals to compile a list of the hundred greatest American films made from 1896 through 1996, and *Citizen Kane* was chosen by more voters than any other. Every ten years since 1952, the film magazine *Sight and Sound* has polled film critics to determine the best films of all time and the ones that stand the test of time despite changing opinions. *Citizen Kane* has topped the list five of the six times the poll was taken.

In his study *The Cinema of Orson Welles,* Peter Cowie writes that *Citizen Kane* "remains Welles' finest film, a treasury of cinematic metaphors and devices, and a portrait of an incredibly powerful personality." He adds that "it will remain one of the few films of which the long-term influence on the history of the cinema was as remarkable as its initial impact."

Welles's later career was spotty. There were some successes like *The Lady From Shanghai, Touch of Evil,* and *Chimes at Midnight,* but producers were generally afraid to put up money for his unusual productions, and he spent many years doing acting jobs to try to raise the capital to make the films he wanted.

Orson Welles died in 1985 at the age of seventy, still considered a genius and still known primarily as the man who made the amazing *Citizen Kane.*

SAM'S BEST YEARS

1944–1946

The war was coming to a close. In Europe the German and Italian armies were suffering defeat after defeat, and soon—on May 8, 1945—victory would be declared in Europe. Just three months later, the Japanese would surrender. In no time hundreds of thousands of servicemen would be headed home, and one question would hang in the air for virtually all of them: Would the transition back to civilian life be an easy one?

Many had been away from home for years, living a very different life from the one they had led before. Would the officer who had commanded hundreds of troops on the battlefield be able to resume a life sitting behind a desk? Would the machine gunner who had killed numerous enemy soldiers be able to resume a simple, peaceful life working in a gas station? Would the man who had survived an enemy prison camp be able to accept a calm, ordinary existence in an urban environment? And most important of all, would the wives and girlfriends still be there after so long?

Frances Goldwyn, the wife of film producer Samuel Goldwyn, had just read a *Time* magazine article that dealt with that very subject, and she suggested the idea to her husband as the theme for a possible film. At first he resisted, but then began to think better of it—especially if he could find the right writer to do it.

If anything, Sam Goldwyn had always been a Hollywood maverick. Born in Poland in 1879, Shmuel Gelbfisz had, at the age of sixteen, made his way across Europe and all the way to England. Three years later, he either begged, borrowed, or stole enough money for a transatlantic crossing to America—in steerage, the cheapest way.

His name was anglicized to Sam Goldfish upon arrival, and he started his life in America as a glove salesman in New York State. Though he became highly successful, Sam was a go-getter, and selling gloves, though profitable, was not a job he wanted to do forever. He convinced theatrical producer Jesse Lasky, whose sister he had married, to start a film-production company, and hired fledgling playwright Cecil B. DeMille. In 1914 their company would produce the first feature film made in Hollywood, *The Squaw Man,* and the company would, many years later, become Paramount Pictures.

When the partnership dissolved, Sam joined with the Selwyn brothers to set up what they called the Goldwyn Company, taking the first syllable of Goldfish and the last syllable of Selwyn. Sam liked the name and decided to change his own name to Goldwyn. Eventually they would merge their studio with the Metro Company and, after other mergers, would become Metro-Goldwyn-Mayer. Ironically, Sam Goldwyn was pushed out before the merger, and although his name was forever attached to the company, he was never actually a part of it.

Goldwyn decided that partnerships resulted in nothing but trouble, and resolved to create a production company that he alone would control. Thus the Goldwyn Company was born. He mostly produced comedies, but in 1944, when he decided to make the film about the returning servicemen, he knew he had a serious and sensitive project on his hands.

Goldwyn hired writer MacKinlay Kantor to develop a story, and Kantor eventually produced a novel titled *Glory for Me,* which was written totally in blank verse. Sam Goldwyn didn't think much of it and set it aside. But when director William Wyler returned from the war and told Sam he was interested in doing something serious, Goldwyn showed him Kantor's book, and the director liked it. Soon Pulitzer Prize–winning writer Robert Sherwood got involved, and he and Wyler were given the go-ahead by Goldwyn to work on a script.

Utilizing Kantor's basic story, which follows three returning veterans who encounter many difficulties as they attempt to adjust to civilian life, Sherwood made one major change. In the original book, one returning vet was disabled by spastic paralysis from shell shock. Instead, he decided to make this character, named Homer, an amputee and found non-actor Harold Russell, who had lost both his hands when a dynamite charge exploded during a training exercise. Casting an amputee in a major role was, in 1945, a risky decision, but Homer would prove to be a character that many returning vets and their families could easily empathize with.

Sherwood worked on the screenplay, eventually delivering the finished script on April 9, 1946. It was twice the length of a normal script, and Sherwood had come up with a new title from a line spoken by one of the characters, *The Best Years of Our Lives.* It was much more than a story of returning veterans—it was a timeless drama about love, marriage, relationships, and the frustrations and challenges of life.

With a cast that included Dana Andrews, Virginia Mayo, Fredric March, and Myrna Loy, and with cinematography by Gregg

Toland (who had filmed Orson Welles's *Citizen Kane*), it took more than a hundred days to shoot. Director Wyler had had the costume designer, Irene Sharaff, go with the actors to department stores and buy clothing that might have been bought by the characters in the film—and wear the clothes before the shooting. He also insisted that the film be made in black and white, which he felt would be more realistic than the look of a Technicolor film, which people associated with musicals and epic dramas.

After editing and scoring, the film ran two hours and forty minutes, almost twice as long as the average ninety-minute films of the time. But when they ran the picture for preview audiences, they quickly discovered that there was virtually no place they could cut it. Viewers were totally enthralled (during some scenes they even stopped chewing their gum!), and when the film ended, it often produced spontaneous applause.

The Best Years of Our Lives opened in Los Angeles and New York on Christmas week of 1946, and the reviews were exceptional. *Variety,* the theatrical tabloid, called it "one of the best pictures of our lives." The *New York Times* said the film "sets the highest standards of cinematic quality and meets them triumphantly," and *Newsweek* called it "epic" art. In its first year of release, the film grossed almost $10 million, making it the second-largest moneymaker in talking picture history. Only *Gone With the Wind* had earned more.

Sam Goldwyn, despite producing almost eighty films in his career, had never won an Academy Award, and as the date approached for the Oscar ceremony, he did not feel optimistic. In spite of his film's great reviews and huge popular success, he was up against several studio-made pictures, and it was common for studio personnel to vote as a block and support their own productions. The awards event had been moved to the vast Shrine Auditorium, seating close to seven thousand people, and tickets had been made available to the public.

On the night of March 13, 1947, the huge assembled crowd saw *The Best Years of Our Lives* run away with award after award. Danny Mandell, editor of the film, took home an award; Hugo Friedhofer won for his music score; Robert Sherwood took Best Screenplay; William Wyler won Best Director; Harold Russell beat out veteran Hollywood performers to get the Best Supporting Actor Oscar; and Fredric March won for Best Actor. When the Best Picture winner was announced, Sam Goldwyn was ecstatic as he danced up the aisle to receive the statuette. He was also given an additional award, the Irving Thalberg Award, for the "most consistent high quality production that year."

That night amputee Harold Russell accomplished something no other actor before or since has achieved by winning two Oscars for the same role, receiving an additional special Academy Award "for bringing hope and courage to his fellow veterans through his appearance in *The Best Years of Our Lives.*"

The evening was a resounding success for Sam Goldwyn, the only sour note being his relationship with director Wyler. The two had argued ferociously during production, and Wyler was determined not to work for Goldwyn again. Unfortunately, despite Sam's entreaties, this would be the case for the remainder of the careers of these two very strong-willed filmmakers.

THE HUAC AND
THE HOLLYWOOD TEN

1947

It could have been a Hollywood drama, but it wasn't. It did have a large, well-known cast of characters. It was part comedy but, for many, a horrible tragedy. Much of it took place in Hollywood, but a good part also took place on location in Washington, D.C.

Its first dramatic moment occurred in a congressional hearing room in Washington on October 20, 1947, as Congressman J. Parnell Thomas opened hearings about Communists in the film industry. But the story had really begun in Hollywood many years before.

In the early 1930s two organizations were created to give Hollywood professionals some control over their jobs: the Screen Writers Guild (SWG) and the Screen Actors Guild (SAG). Although originally formed in 1921, the Screen Writers Guild began to gain strength in 1933, and by 1937 (after the Supreme Court found the National Labor Relations Act to be constitutional), the writers began to organize to gain collective bargaining in the movie industry. Eventually an agreement was signed with the studios in 1942.

In March 1933 six actors organized the Screen Actors Guild, which over the years grew to a membership of four thousand. The National Labor Relations Act set the stage in 1937 for SAG to negotiate with the film producers.

Among the many reasons for the formation of the two guilds was to give writers and actors some means of negotiating contracts with the studios. For many years studio bosses kept their writers and actors under tight control, forcing them to abide by strict contracts the studios had written and dictating their salaries and the films they could work on. The studio heads resented any possible independence for their workers and sometimes tried to force them out of the guilds—often by threats. But both the SWG (which would ultimately become the Writers Guild of America or WGA) and SAG continued to gain strength.

Many of the individuals who ran the studios believed the hierarchies of these guilds—especially that of the writers—were infiltrated by Communists, and there were indeed guild members who were members of the Communist Party. It must be stressed, however, that membership in the Communist Party, like most political organizations, was (and is) definitely not illegal.

In 1938 a congressional committee chaired by Texas congressman Martin Dies was formed to expose Communist conspiracies. Dies told the press that Hollywood was a hotbed of Communism and, in 1939, the Dies Committee began hearings at the Hollywood Roosevelt Hotel. Congressman Dies accused numerous Hollywood figures of being Communists, but almost all proved that his allegations were totally false.

By 1941 the United States had entered World War II, and the enemies were now Germany, Japan, and Fascism. For the time being, the Russians became our friends. However, once the Fascists were defeated, there was a sudden awareness that the Russians had major intentions of taking over many Eastern European countries and making Communism a dominant political ideology wherever they could. In March 1946 British Prime Minister Winston Churchill made his famous speech declaring that an "Iron Curtain" had descended across Europe. The Russians and their Communist principles had now become the enemy of America's democratic way of life.

The Dies Committee was soon supplanted by the House Committee on Un-American Activities, or HUAC. And the HUAC clearly made its intentions known: to investigate Hollywood to show that the movie community was infested with Communists, and to prove that many films were clearly full of anti-American propaganda. Suddenly Hollywood was divided into "friendly" witnesses, who claimed to be eager to root out anyone in the film industry who might be Communist, and "unfriendly" witnesses, who felt that the committee's basic philosophy and its methods were clearly illegal and unconstitutional.

Using information supplied to them by the FBI, the HUAC in September 1947 issued subpoenas to forty-three people in the Hollywood community to appear at a hearing in October in Washington. First to be interviewed were "friendly" witnesses like studio boss Jack Warner. Next came a group of "concerned patriotic citizens" that included actors Gary Cooper and Ronald Reagan. These two groups were outspoken in naming names and accusing others of being Communists.

Finally, nineteen individuals were named who would be known as "unfriendly" witnesses. First to be quizzed was writer John Howard Lawson. Lawson was known to have been a member of the Communist Party and was also a former president of the Screen Writers Guild. His interview proved to be a shouting match with HUAC chairman J. Parnell Thomas. Lawson kept trying to make a statement, but Thomas kept refusing to allow him to do it. Ultimately,

Lawson was forcibly removed from the room. Nine more of the unfriendly witnesses were called, and all refused to answer the committee's questions. They cited the First Amendment, insisting that it gave them "freedom of speech," and that Congress could not abridge this freedom. The group's intention was to cast aspersions at the HUAC, but the questioning frequently deteriorated into shouting matches between the committee and those being interviewed.

This was the group that became known as the "Hollywood Ten." They were writers Alvah Bessie, Lester Cole, Ring Lardner Jr., John Howard Lawson, Abert Maltz, Samuel Ornitz, and Dalton Trumbo. The group also included producer Adrian Scott and the directors Edward Dmytryk and Herbert Biberman. Their refusal to cooperate with the HUAC would soon have them cited for the crime of "contempt of Congress." The committee abruptly ended its hearings after only ten days—but this was only the beginning.

Less than a month after the hearings ended, a group of Hollywood producers met at the Waldorf Astoria Hotel in New York and drafted a statement saying that they supported the HUAC, would not employ the Hollywood Ten, and would weed out any other subversives in their industry and refuse to employ them. It was the beginning of what would become the "blacklist."

Suddenly the Hollywood Ten could not get work, and many others who were merely suspected of being Communists or Communist sympathizers found themselves out of a job and unable to get hired. The Hollywood Ten fought their contempt citations through the courts, but ultimately, in April 1950, the U.S. Supreme Court denied them a hearing and they were sent to prison. Eight were given a year's sentence, and two served six months.

One of the great ironies was that shortly after the Ten had been cited for contempt, the chairman of the committee that had held them in contempt, J. Parnell Thomas, was himself convicted of fraud for using government funds for his own personal use and was sent to the federal prison at Danbury, Connecticut—the very same prison where writers Ring Lardner and Lester Cole were serving time!

In March 1951 the HUAC reconvened its hearings, and more and more witnesses were called. By this time a great wave of fear had spread among those in Hollywood. Now witnesses admitted their indiscretions, and many named others who, they said, were Communists or sympathizers with Communist principles. By doing this, they claimed they were hardly causing harm since the committee already knew of most of those accused. Yet, when they cooperated with the HUAC, jobs suddenly opened up for them. On the other hand, they forged a permanent enmity with those who had stuck by their principles.

Many talented writers who had been put on the blacklist continued to write and submitted scripts under false names. They also employed "fronts," people who would claim to be the writer of the script, even though almost everyone knew who the real author was.

The results of the blacklist were tragic for many. Several individuals committed suicide, notably Philip Loeb, who had had a regular part on the TV series *The Goldbergs* but could no longer get work. Some, such as writer Dalton Trumbo and director Jules Dassin, left the country and worked abroad. Writers on the blacklist who were hired surreptitiously were taken advantage of and paid much less than their normal salaries. Hollywood abounded with fear, dishonesty, hatred, and anger—and it lasted well into the 1950s.

Living and working in Mexico, blacklisted writer Dalton Trumbo wrote a script in 1956 about a boy and a bull. He was able to interest some producers in making the film, and it was eventually produced with the title *The Brave One*. Since Trumbo could not use his own name, he went by "Robert Rich." When the Academy Awards were given out in 1956, the Best Film Story award went to

. . . Robert Rich! Another writer accepted the award for "Rich," but soon there was a scramble to find out who Rich really was. At first Trumbo was evasive, but eventually it was discovered who had written the screenplay.

The blacklist had begun to crumble, but it still existed. In a bravura attempt to stop the blacklisting, Trumbo made offers to various producers to write a script for no salary—if they would put his name on the screen as the writer. Since he was able to make as much as $75,000 for a screenplay, this was an amazing offer, but fear still existed in the industry, and there were no takers.

When Trumbo was hired by actor Kirk Douglas to write the screenplay for *Spartacus,* a film that would be produced by his company, Bryna, the Trumbo name was still an obstacle, so it was decided he would use the name "Sam Jackson." But when he completed work on the *Spartacus* script and was hired by director Otto Preminger to do a rewrite of the script for the novel *Exodus,* Preminger was not afraid to let it be publicly known that the writer to be credited was Dalton Trumbo. The deception was now over: Trumbo's name appeared on both films, and, in many ways, the blacklist had ended.

In November 1960 John F. Kennedy was elected president. Before he took office, Kennedy and his brother Robert went to a Washington, D.C., theater to see *Spartacus.* Outside the theater, pickets paraded, protesting the fact that Dalton Trumbo, one of the infamous Hollywood Ten, had written the film. Undeterred, John and Robert Kennedy crossed the picket line and went to the movies.

THE STUDIO SYSTEM
BEGINS TO FADE

1949–1954

For many years they controlled everything. They put their actors under contract and told them which pictures they could appear in, and would often loan their contract players out to other studios for a fee. They controlled the writers and the directors, and decided which films would be made, often monitoring every aspect of each production. They even owned the theaters where the films were shown.

They were the Hollywood studios, and they had a virtual stranglehold on everything connected with moviemaking for more than forty years. The men who ran the studios called all the shots, but as the 1940s came to a close, things were going to change—and the change would be a dramatic one. It was all caused not by one factor, but by a series of events, legal decisions, and popular behavior.

One factor was demographics. The war was over, the troops had come home, and their babies were being born with a vengeance. The "baby boom" was occurring, and couples were staying home rather than going to the movies. In just a few years television would be available to anyone who could afford a set, and entertainment, sports, and news would come into homes for free. As Sam Goldwyn put it in his most characteristic way, "Why should people pay money to see lousy movies when they can watch lousy television at home for free?"

Then came the court decisions: In 1949 the Supreme Court ruled in *United States vs. Paramount, Inc.* that studio ownership of theaters constituted an illegal monopoly. By 1954 all the studios had divested themselves of ownership in movie houses, and theater owners could now negotiate for the films they wanted to show without being forced to present movies the studios chose for them.

Another legal factor was the Olivia de Havilland decision, which affected many studio contract players. A popular actress who had starred in many films (including playing the role of Melanie in *Gone With the Wind*), she was under contract to Warner Brothers Studio. But when her seven-year contract ended and she thought she was free of studio control, Miss de Havilland was informed that since she had had a half-year suspension during the life of the contract, she still owed the studio six months. She refused and took the studio to court. The case ultimately wound up in the California Supreme Court, which ruled in her favor. This decision also affected actors who had served in the war who were being told they still had obligations to fulfill their contracts. Apparently, patriotism took a backseat for the studio bosses who wanted control over their stars, but the "de Havilland Decision" worked in favor of the returning veterans, and many were now free of their contracts. The studios were beginning to lose their tight control over their performers.

Then, in 1951, came the fall of a major studio icon: Louis B. Mayer. He had run Metro-Goldwyn-Mayer since the thirties and, to many, seemed to be the most powerful figure in all of Hollywood. But even he was vulnerable, and in a power struggle he lost control of the studio to his head of production, Dore Schary.

Many movie stars were not under contract anymore and could negotiate on their own or, as usually happened, through their agents. Now agents like MCA (Music Corporation of America), which represented many actors, could put together deals involving their clients. Much of the control of moviemaking had taken a major shift.

Then came the coup de grâce: the invasion of the small screen. Audiences began staying at home, and movie attendance declined rapidly. Some in the film business saw the writing on the wall and tried to come up with movies that would pull people away from the little black-and-white screen. First it was musicals in color, providing the size and scope TV watchers could not experience at home. Films that are now considered classics of the genre, like *Annie Get Your Gun, An American in Paris,* and *Singin' in the Rain,* brought audiences back to the theaters—for a time.

Then came specialty films, with reserved seating, to make movie-going a special event, like going to see a stage play. Most prominent of these was showman Mike Todd's adaptation of the Jules Verne novel *Around the World in Eighty Days,* a two-and-a-half-hour-long (with intermission) movie featuring dozens of stars in cameo parts.

Other devices used to lure audiences away from their TV sets included special film technologies. Three-dimensional films that required wearing Polaroid glasses were popular for a few years, then slipped into obscurity (until the 1990s, when the basic 3-D technique was used successfully in some of the giant-screen IMAX films shown in specially designed theaters around the country). Perhaps the most successful novel technology, for a time anyway, was Cinerama. Originally introduced for the travelogue *This Is Cinerama,* it involved making a movie using three cameras, then projecting it on a huge screen with three synchronized projectors.

More wide-screen techniques soon followed, and by the 1960s and '70s the almost-square screen of the past was replaced by the wider image most people now see in their local theaters. Interestingly, even the television image has now gone "wide screen," with flat screens now the norm and the wider image easily able to show modern feature films without having to adapt them, as was formerly needed with the almost-square TV screen.

The big studios had had their day, and films were now being packaged by agents and lawyers, often with the major stars themselves having veto power over script, other performers, choice of director, and virtually all aspects of the production. The studios were now just places for independent film producers to rent facilities, and distribution outlets for the films being made.

As this happened, the composition of the moviegoing audience began to change as well. In the thirties, forties, and fifties, movie attendance was frequently a family affair, and the Production Code rigidly controlled the language and subject matter of films. But by the sixties the code was replaced by movie ratings and the appeal was now to a younger audience. There was more violence on the screen (and quite graphic violence), four-letter words became the norm, and sex and sexual situations were now freely portrayed.

Movie admission fees gradually rose, and even the prices at the refreshment stand escalated. Many people were literally priced out of the theaters.

Finally came the explosion of movies on videocassettes, followed by digital video discs (DVDs). More and more the viewing audience was watching movies at home, not on the tiny black-and-white screens of the early days of television, but on huge home screens with images almost as sharp as those they could watch at the local multiplex theater.

The demise of the studio system in the late 1940s was the beginning of a big change in Hollywood—and many additional changes would lie ahead.

THE STRANGE DEATH
OF A GODDESS

1962

Her naked body lay stretched out on the bed. One hand was extended, as if it were reaching for the telephone at the bedside. Her housekeeper, Mrs. Eunice Murray, noticed the strange position and called psychiatrist Dr. Ralph R. Greenson. He quickly arrived and broke a pane of glass in the French window, opened the door, and found her unconscious. Dr. Greenson called her physician, Dr. Hyman Engelberg, who arrived and pronounced her dead. Finally, the police were called.

The woman who lay on the bed was Marilyn Monroe. She was thirty-six years old.

Since that early-August morning in 1962, there has been much speculation about the death of the Hollywood sex goddess whose film appearances had created a huge following among the moviegoing public and both admiration and anger from those who worked with her. Was her death a suicide? Or was she really murdered? Were there powerful people who might have been responsible? Was there a major cover-up of the facts?

One thing, however, is certain: The years that led up to that fatal morning had been a roller coaster ride of ups and downs for the actress, a woman who had hobnobbed with the rich and famous, and who had endured much pain in her brief thirty-six years.

Norma Jeane Mortenson was born June 1, 1926, in Los Angeles. Her mother was Gladys Pearl Monroe Mortenson, and her father, who deserted his wife before Norma Jeane was born, was Martin Edward Mortenson. Gladys would spend a good deal of time in mental hospitals, and the child would spend much of her early life being shuffled between foster homes, orphanages, and relatives' houses.

To escape this insecure life, at the age of sixteen Norma Jeane married Jim Dougherty, who in 1944 joined the merchant marines and was sent overseas. While her husband was away, she worked in a defense plant and, by chance, had her photo taken by an army photographer. The sexual energy was obvious in the photograph, and soon she was hired to do other photo shoots for a variety of girlie magazines.

In 1946 four important things happened that would change her life forever: She decided to divorce Jim Dougherty, she dyed her hair blonde, and she was offered a contract with Twentieth Century Fox. She also changed her name to one that would soon be known the world over: Marilyn Monroe.

The sexual image that was pervasive in her still photos was even more pronounced in her film roles. In the six years that followed, she appeared in eighteen films under various studio contracts, mostly in small roles. But by 1953 she was acknowledged as a movie star, as she was cast in major roles in *Niagara, Gentlemen Prefer Blondes,* and *How to Marry a Millionaire.* Her second marriage—to baseball star Joe DiMaggio—lasted less than a year.

Although she had signed a seven-year contract with Twentieth Century Fox and was committed to appearing in films they assigned her to make, she left both the studio and Hollywood for New York. She was tired of playing the stereotypical "dumb blonde" and wanted to do some serious acting work. In New York she studied with Lee Strasberg at his famous Actors Studio, where the emphasis was on "method acting," getting to the soul of the character you were playing and giving more than just a surface performance.

Marilyn returned to Hollywood to make *Bus Stop* in 1956, with a performance that was hailed by critics. But though her professional life had taken a leap forward, her personal life had not. She was using various drugs and drinking excessively. Her behavior on the set was difficult and erratic. In June 1956 she married playwright Arthur Miller—the award-winning author of many highly regarded plays, including *Death of a Salesman, All My Sons,* and *The Crucible*—and in 1959 appeared in the highly successful comedy *Some Like It Hot.*

But her problems with drugs, alcohol, and depression—as well as several miscarriages—continued to take a heavy toll. Her playwright husband had written a screenplay for a film called *The Misfits,* in which she had a major role. Not long after the film was released, she and Miller divorced, and, distraught, she entered the Payne Whitney Psychiatric Clinic in New York. Her treatment, however, proved only transitory, and she was soon experiencing frequent ups and downs and relying on pills and alcohol.

In 1962 she purchased a modest one-story bungalow in the community of Brentwood, west of Hollywood. She was scheduled to begin filming *Something's Got to Give* with Dean Martin at Twentieth Century Fox, but her behavior on the set was erratic and she was often absent, claiming she was ill. It was during this period that she suddenly showed up in New York during a birthday celebration for president John F. Kennedy at Madison Square Garden. Marilyn stepped to the microphone and, staring directly up at the president's box, sang "Happy Birthday." She appeared to have more than just admiration for the president as she sang—there seemed to be an effusion of major affection that came from her as the simple song was sung.

Rumors about her possible romantic relationship with the president, as well as his brother Robert, had long been circulated. But were the rumors true? Many authors have verified that Marilyn and John Kennedy had had a brief sexual relationship, and there is also ample evidence that she and Robert had also been lovers. In both cases the men had ended the relationship without even saying good-bye, and in both cases she had felt ill-used.

Some authors have even speculated that the Kennedys had a hand in her death, or that her relationship with them had made her vulnerable to those who feared or hated them. However, the official story (supplied by Twentieth Century Fox) was that housekeeper Eunice Murray noticed Marilyn's light on at 3:30 in the morning, and she did not respond when Murray knocked on her door. Murray ran outside to look through the window and saw Marilyn on the bed "looking strange." She phoned Dr. Greenson (her psychiatrist), who arrived at 3:40 a.m. and broke into the bedroom and found her dead. Dr. Engelberg (her physician) arrived and officially pronounced her dead at 4:00 a.m. Reports said that Marilyn Monroe had died from "accidental suicide."

Five days later the Los Angeles County coroner described the cause of death as "the result of barbiturate poisoning, specifically of Nembutal and chloral hydrate." There remain, however, many unanswered questions about the strange death of the Hollywood goddess, among them: Why were the phone records of her calls the night before she died confiscated? And why were all the letters and documents from her home taken and destroyed?

There has been, over the years, much speculation that because Marilyn Monroe had been ill-treated by John and Robert Kennedy, she was on the verge of telling the press about the relationships, and this may have led to her death. Two books postulate this theory with ample evidence of the cover-up of the real story behind her death, *The Curious Death of Marilyn Monroe* by Robert F. Slatzer and *Marilyn: The Last Take* by Peter Harry Brown and Patte B. Barham. In addition, Anthony Summers's book *Goddess: The Secret Lives of Marilyn Monroe* details her complex relationship with the Kennedy brothers.

Unfortunately, with most of those involved no longer alive and with many relevant records destroyed, we will probably never know the truth about her death. As with so many mysteries, a lot of questions about the death of Marilyn will continue to remain unanswered.

A HILLSIDE MANSION BECOMES
A MAGICAL PLACE

1963

He could see the old Hollywood mansion from his office on the ninth floor. Weeds grew in the front yard, and it looked as if no one had lived there for a very long time. It definitely resembled something from a horror movie.

His name was Milt Larsen, and he was a television writer for Ralph Edwards Productions. He was also a part-time magician and loved hobnobbing with those who practiced sleight of hand. His father, William Larsen, had given up a successful law practice to tour with his magic show, and, of course, his kids quickly became part of the act. But then his father died at the age of forty-eight, and he and his brother Bill became involved in the television business, Milt as a gag writer for *Truth or Consequences* and Bill as an associate producer at CBS-TV. But magic was in their blood, and they published a magazine for magicians called *Genii*.

Milt had always envisioned some kind of club as a meeting place for magicians. He and a friend named Don Gotschall had even

considered buying a San Francisco ferryboat that was for sale, bringing it (somehow) to Marina del Rey, renovating it into a showboat,
and operating it as a vaudeville theater. When they discovered all the
potential costs involved, however, they quickly scrapped the idea.

But now twenty-nine-year-old Milt Larsen was staring down
at the dilapidated building on Franklin Avenue and wondering if,
maybe, there was a possibility that this place, with a bit of work,
could be transformed into a magic castle. Built in 1909 by banker
and real estate magnate Rollin B. Lane, the building was occupied
by the Lane family for more than thirty years. Lane had planned to
develop the many acres of Hollywood he owned into orange groves
and ranches, but a severe drought ruined his plans and he was unable
to sell much of the property. The Lane family moved away, and the
mansion was sold and later used as a home for the elderly. Still later,
it became an apartment house.

By 1960 the new owner, Thomas O. Glover, was not sure what
to do with the mansion. Then Milt Larsen decided to approach him
with an idea. They met in September 1961 and shook hands over a
simple agreement: Milt could have the building rent-free for a year
and could do any renovations he wanted. If he did get it into a condi-
tion where it could function as a club, Tom would get a percentage
of the food and bar sales. Milt's dream of a magicians' club was now
on the road to becoming a reality—but it would be a long road, with
many setbacks along the way.

Along with a lawyer friend named Bob Post (who volunteered his
services), Milt, brother Bill, and Ron Gotschall set up an organization
called the Academy of Magical Arts, Inc. Then they tried to get as
many of their friends as they could to become members. They charged
a membership fee of $35 for magicians and $25 for non-magicians.

When they posted a notice in the window of their intent to sell
alcohol under the aegis of their "Academy of Magical Arts," the local

citizenry, apparently assuming the place was about to be inhabited by witches and warlocks, tried to block their permit. However, Milt and Bill talked to the locals and were able to convince them that they were responsible members of the community, and the license was ultimately granted.

Milt now embarked on the massive job of redoing the interior. This included the laborious task of removing paint from the beautiful hardwood, going through two gallons of paint remover a week and employing lots of elbow grease. Luckily, he discovered that some old Los Angeles mansions were in the process of being demolished, so, for a mere $900, he got permission to remove anything he could from one of them before the wrecker's ball descended. Thus he became the owner, for two weeks, of a million-dollar mansion and, with some friends, made regular trips to remove panels, windows, molding, etc.—leaving little more for the wrecking crew than the outer shell.

Soon Milt found people who could help him find used items that would become part of the castle he was creating. Carpeting, woodwork, and beautiful cabinetry salvaged from buildings about to go under the wrecking ball ended up being taken to Franklin Avenue.

Two of the fascinating features of the Magic Castle (even today) were designed in its earliest days. One is the "Open Sesame" bookcase. When guests arrive, they utter the magic words "Open Sesame," and a bookcase swings open to admit them. Milt's friend Spencer Quinn helped design the entranceway using a system of ropes and pulleys that would open the bookcase when a lever was triggered by the hostess's foot.

"Irma," the invisible piano player, continues to enchant Castle visitors. Today she is in the room behind the first-floor bar and plays requested songs, with the keys going down even though no one is apparently playing. In Milt and Spencer's original design, a live pianist played in one room and his keyboard opened valves on a player piano in the room where guests were present. The original pianist, Bill Groom, would play for the guests, then take a break, allowing invisible "Irma" to take over. However, the guests enjoyed Irma much more than a real pianist, and Groom enjoyed being away from the visitors (especially if they requested songs he didn't know), so the invisible performer became a permanent fixture. Incidentally, the piano has been relocated from its original spot and the technique employed to make it play is now a closely guarded secret.

The Magic Castle had its official opening at 6:00 p.m. on January 2, 1963. The opening was only salvaged, as far as drinks were concerned, by a friend of Milt's who had a liquor store. The Castle's liquor license had only been approved that afternoon, and his friend brought the appropriate bottles, just in time, at 5:00 p.m.!

Over the years the Magic Castle has grown and expanded— almost like magic. In reality, it is all the result of hard work by Milt, along with many others. Today there is a large showroom with a stage, the Palace of Mystery, which opened in 1974; a smaller theater named the Parlor of Prestidigitation; and several smaller rooms on the lower level. The Magic Castle also has an excellent restaurant and now boasts five bars, and it has become a popular place for parties and celebrations.

Since only a limited number of visitors can be accommodated at a time, attendance is restricted to members or those invited by members. Membership is available to magicians, who must pass an initiation performance, and to "associate members," who are only required to have a love and appreciation of the magical arts.

The old mansion on Hollywood's Franklin Avenue has come a long way over the years, evolving into a world-famous club that attracts some of magic's great performers. Milt Larsen's vision, hard work, and creativity made a dream become an amazing reality.

THE TRAGIC DEATH OF
A SILENT-SCREEN IDOL

1968

He was almost seventy years old. He had been a dashingly handsome leading man in the films of the 1920s and '30s, but since then his career had had a series of ups and downs. It all ended on the morning of October 31, 1968, when police found the nude body of Ramon Novarro lying dead on his bed, his body covered with bruises, his ankles and wrists tied with electric cords.

He was born Ramon Gil Samaneigo in 1899 in the town of Durango, Mexico. His father was a respected dentist, but when Ramon was just eleven, with the Huerta Revolution erupting, the family fled to Mexico City. In 1917 they moved again, this time to Los Angeles.

While still a young man, Ramon was forced to become the head of the household when his father became seriously ill. He worked at an assortment of jobs, from theater usher to hotel busboy, but his skills in music enabled him to give piano lessons and work in a cafe as a singing waiter. His strikingly handsome appearance got him some bit parts in movies. He appeared in Mack Sennett's *A Small Town*

Idol in 1921, doing a dance wearing a loincloth, and had a bit part in *The Four Horsemen of the Apocalypse* (also in 1921), a film that starred the popular Rudolph Valentino. The director of this film was Rex Ingram, who decided to give young Ramon a bigger role in a film he was doing based on the novel *The Prisoner of Zenda.* He also suggested he change his name to Ramon Novarro.

The film was a popular success, and Ramon's role as a swash-buckling villain, complete with beard, monocle, and long cigarette holder, quickly earned him popularity with audiences. Director Ingram signed him to a personal contract at $125 per week and cast him in a series of pictures that soon raised him to stardom. The first was *Where the Rainbow Ends* (1923), as a native boy in love with a missionary's daughter, followed by major parts in *Scaramouche* (1923) and *The Arab* (1924).

Novarro had now advanced to the rank of major Hollywood matinee idol along with Rudolph Valentino and John Gilbert. Tragically, in 1926 the thirty-one-year-old Valentino died from peritonitis triggered by a ruptured appendix. Just a few years later, Gilbert's star would fade, in part due to his poor voice quality for sound films.

In 1925 Novarro was given the lead role in the biblical drama *Ben-Hur.* The film had started production in Italy with George Walsh in the leading role, but it had encountered a myriad of problems and a vast amount of money was wasted. MGM decided to cancel production in Italy, move the film back to Hollywood, and replace both the director and the star. The picture still wound up costing almost $6 million (probably the most expensive film made up to that time), but it proved to be a major box office success. Novarro was a sensation—especially with female audiences, mostly due to the brief costumes he wore that revealed his masculine anatomy.

Ironically, in spite of the romantic roles he would play and the many lovely actresses he dated, Ramon Novarro was more interested in men and was known to have numerous male lovers, including author and adventurer Richard Halliburton. It was rumored that MGM's Louis Mayer had tried on numerous occasions to convince Novarro to marry (for the sake of appearances), but the actor had always refused.

Novarro's career continued to blossom with *The Student Prince in Old Heidelberg* (1927) opposite Norma Shearer; *Across to Singapore* (1928) with Joan Crawford; and his first talkie, *Devil May Care* (1929), in which he played a singing French soldier. As his career hit its peak, he was earning as much as $100,000 per film. He built a seventeen-room mansion and invited several members of his family to live with him. He also invested wisely in real estate, including purchasing a fifty-acre ranch near San Diego.

Novarro made two films in the early 1930s: *Mata Hari* in 1931 with Greta Garbo, and *The Barbarian* in 1934 with Myrna Loy. By 1935, however, his contract with MGM had ended and was not renewed. He toured with his sister Carmen in South America and Europe doing theater, then produced and directed a Spanish-language feature film in 1936 called *Contra la Corriente*.

As the years passed, he would appear occasionally in bit parts in feature films, mostly doing character roles, and he also did some touring in summer stock productions. The last film he made was *Heller in Pink Tights* in 1960, though he occasionally appeared on television throughout the sixties.

Apparently Novarro was financially secure, but personally went through periods of depression and guilt because of his homosexuality. He drank a good deal and was stopped by police on a number of occasions for driving under the influence of alcohol.

When the police were called to Novarro's Hollywood Hills home by his secretary, Edward Weber, that October night in 1968, they found the living room a total shambles and the bedroom a virtual bloodbath. Not only was his nude body covered with bruises and his ankles and wrists tied with electric cord, but there was a zigzag mark on his neck. Scribbled on the sheet under his body was the name "Larry."

Larry turned out to be a friend (or perhaps former lover) who had told his brother-in-law, Paul Ferguson, that Novarro very likely had several thousand dollars stashed in the house. Twenty-two-year-old Paul and his seventeen-year-old brother, Tom, made contact with Novarro and agreed to come to his place for an assignation—in exchange for cash. The brothers arrived at about 5:30 p.m., and they all began drinking. Paul, however, soon became violent and began to beat Novarro until he was bloody. When the actor regained consciousness, Paul again beat him with a riding cane, and Novarro fell to the floor and suffocated in his own blood.

The two brothers then dragged Novarro to the bed, tied his hands, and scrawled "Larry" on the sheet—apparently to direct the blame away from them. The only money they found in the house was $45. At Novarro's funeral, on November 4, 1968, more than a thousand people passed his coffin, and he was buried at Calvary Cemetery in Los Angeles.

Police were able to trace a phone call that one of the brothers had made from Novarro's house the night of the murder, as well as identify fingerprints found in the room. The Ferguson brothers were arrested on November 6, 1968—just a week after the killing—and were soon tried for murder. The trial lasted six and a half weeks, and they were both convicted and sentenced to life terms. They served several years but were released on parole, only to soon wind up back in prison when they were arrested for rape.

Ramon Novarro is remembered by a star on the Hollywood Walk of Fame (at 6350 Hollywood Boulevard); two biographies, Allan Ellenberger's *Ramon Novarro* and Andre Soares's *Beyond Paradise: The Life of Ramon Novarro*; a short story by Charles Bukowski, "The Murder of Ramon Vasquez"; and a play by George Barthel, *Through a Naked Lens,* that was produced in New York in 2005.

DRUGS, MOTORCYCLES, FONDA, AND HOPPER

1969

For many in America, the sixties were the decade of "tune in, turn on, and drop out." There were protests against the Vietnam War, sit-ins at schools and colleges, marches in the streets, and an active and outspoken youth movement. It was also the decade in which John F. Kennedy, his brother Robert, and civil rights leader Martin Luther King were all assassinated. And it was the decade that saw the rapid spread of the drug culture.

In Hollywood, very few films mirrored this youth movement—that is, until a wild and unusual movie was made by two young film-makers. Their names were Peter Fonda and Dennis Hopper, and the movie would eventually be called *Easy Rider*.

Films prominently involving motorcycles were hardly a new phenomenon: Marlon Brando's movie career had begun with 1954's *The Wild One,* and low-budget filmmaker Roger Corman, in 1966, made *The Wild Angels*—starring Peter Fonda. The predominant element of many of the early "biker" films was the motorcycle gang, often spreading destruction in its wake as it roared through small-town America. But when Peter Fonda conceived the idea for his film about two motorcycle buddies riding across the American South, he had something else in mind.

The son of famed actor Henry Fonda, Peter was born in New York in 1939. He entered the University of Omaha at the age of seventeen, did some little theater, then went to New York. On Broadway he was cast in a production of *Blood, Sweat, and Stanley Poole* and shortly after went to Hollywood.

Peter appeared in several films, mostly playing romantic leads, but in private he let his hair grow long and became a true hippie, using drugs and living a counterculture lifestyle. In 1966 he was cast as a biker in Corman's *The Wild Angels,* a violent motorcycle film that involved heavy drug use. In Corman's *The Trip* (1967), the emphasis was totally on the effects of using the drug LSD.

Shortly after *The Trip,* Fonda came up with the idea for *Easy Rider*—a film about two long-haired hippies who make some quick cash from a drug transaction, buy some motorcycles, and then travel across the country. The film would co-star and be directed by his friend Dennis Hopper.

Hopper, born in Dodge City, Kansas, in 1936, studied at the famous Actors Studio in New York and was soon cast in numerous television shows. He appeared in several feature films in the 1960s, including *Cool Hand Luke* with Paul Newman and *True Grit* with John Wayne.

In 1968 Fonda and Hopper brought the idea for the film to young producers Bert Schneider and Bob Rafaelson. Based on the huge success of their TV series *The Monkees* (featuring a young, Beatles-like rock group), Schneider and Rafaelson had become wealthy and respected producers. Originally titled *The Loners,* the film was offbeat enough to appeal to a youthful audience.

The producers liked Fonda's idea—especially when he said they could make the film for less than $400,000. Schneider wrote a personal check for $40,000 so they could do some preliminary shooting while Mardi Gras was occurring. But they got their dates wrong and realized they had just a week to prepare. Quickly they assembled a crew and headed for New Orleans. While they were gone, Schneider convinced Columbia (normally a staid and conservative studio) to take on the picture.

New Orleans proved to be a disaster, primarily because Hopper (now directing his first film) was on a wild ego trip and he and Fonda were constantly at each other's throats. Nevertheless, once they got back, Fonda, Hopper, and writer Terry Southern sat down and worked out a script.

They hired Jack Nicholson for the role of a civil rights lawyer named Hanson who decides to go with them on their journey, put together a crew, had some motorcycles (that were originally police bikes) redesigned, and then headed out to make the movie. They utilized places and people they encountered along the way, and ended up with thousands of feet of film that Hopper originally edited down to a four-hour movie.

Fonda and Hopper were at odds throughout much of the filming, and when Hopper insisted that his four-hour version be the definitive one, Fonda had to get him out of the editing room for a vacation so they could work on cutting the film to a proper length. It was producer Bert Schneider who insisted Hopper go to Taos, New Mexico, for a break, and while he was gone, they recut the film, bringing it down to a workable length.

Ultimately cut to ninety-four minutes, the film had instant appeal to a young movie audience. The themes of antiestablishment behavior, drug use, confrontations with authority, and a pulsating rock-and-roll sound track made *Easy Rider* a huge success.

In essence, the film followed freethinking, freedom-loving Captain America (Fonda) and Billy the Kid (Hopper), soon accompanied by Nicholson, as they traveled across America, being confronted along the way by intolerance, hatred, and fear of the two long-haired bike riders—a hatred that ultimately results in their deaths at the hands of local "rednecks." Fonda and Hopper chose rock music from their own record collections as a temporary sound track but soon realized how effective their choices were, and ultimately (though it took a lot of effort and cajoling to get the rights) this was the music they used.

The movie was shown at film festivals and was an immediate success. They took the film to the Cannes Film Festival, where it won an award for the best movie by a new director. The official opening in the United States was at the Beekman Theater in New York. Word quickly spread, and soon the long-haired, barefooted crowd was lining up for every show—the management even had to take the doors off the bathroom stalls to prevent the audience from smoking pot!

In its first week, in one theater, they made back virtually the entire budget of the film. Soon, in theaters all over the country, young people lined up to see it, many watching it over and over again. *Life* magazine called Hopper "Hollywood's hottest director," and he quickly became a spokesman for the counterculture.

Dennis Hopper, Peter Fonda, and Terry Southern were nominated for an Academy Award for the *Easy Rider* script, but lost to William Goldman and his script for *Butch Cassidy and the Sundance Kid*. Jack Nicholson was nominated as Best Supporting Actor, but lost to Gig Young for *They Shoot Horses, Don't They?* Nicholson would, however, be a winner at numerous future Oscar ceremonies.

Despite the lack of Oscars, the film changed a great many things. The studio system was already gone, but *Easy Rider* shifted the focus of many movies to come. The smaller, independent production now proved it had an audience, and that audience was the youth audience. The executives from Columbia who first saw *Easy Rider* and could not understand its appeal now had to face the fact that a lot was changing in the film business. Unfortunately, this vibrant new youth spirit did not last long.

The sixties were over, and the "season of love" had reached its end. The Vietnam War dragged on despite the protests, and Richard Nixon was reelected. Yet a new crop of filmmakers would soon be on the scene. Perhaps the future successes of the likes of George Lucas, Steven Spielberg, and Francis Ford Coppola would, in many respects, be due to that strange, offbeat, mystical, and overwhelmingly popular production called *Easy Rider*.

DEATH IN THE TWILIGHT ZONE

1982

It was certainly one of the most popular shows on television, and it ran from 1959 to 1965. Hosted by award-winning writer Rod Serling, the series originally consisted of half-hour shows (they were later a full hour), each of which had some aspect of the weird about it and an ironic, twist ending. Television audiences loved the shows, and they were often talked about on the following day at school and at work.

The final episode of the television series aired in September 1965, but in 1982 producer Steven Spielberg and director John Landis decided to resurrect the concept in a feature film. There would be four short episodes, and each, like the TV episodes, would have an unusual ending. Each episode was to be handled by a different director: Landis and Spielberg would each do one, and Joe Dante and George Miller would do the other two.

Landis had worked his way up in the movie business from mail boy at Twentieth Century Fox, then as a stuntman in Europe, dialogue coach, and production assistant. His first directing job, at the age of twenty-one, was for a picture he wrote and even appeared in called *Schlock*. It was not until six years later, in 1977, that his film *Kentucky Fried Movie* (a series of comedy sketches) was made. This was followed by *National Lampoon's Animal House,* another wacky comedy that had great appeal to the youth audience. He then directed the very successful *The Blues Brothers* and, in 1981, the comedy-horror film *An American Werewolf in London.*

Landis decided to write an original script for his episode of *The Twilight Zone* (the other episodes were reworkings of former television pieces), and he wanted it to have some social and moral bite. In his story, a highly outspoken and bigoted man named Bill Connor leaves a bar and suddenly realizes he is in a different time and place, then another, and then another. In each new place he becomes a victim of vicious intolerance: persecuted as a Jew in Nazi-occupied France; pursued by a lynch mob that thinks he is a black man in the American South; and chased by a patrol of American soldiers in Vietnam who think he is a Viet Cong guerilla. Each time he sees the effects of bigotry by being put in the shoes of the victims—he not only sees it, he lives it. In a later rewrite of the script, two Vietnamese children were added, and Connor tries to help them escape the siege of their village by U.S. forces. Landis added this element to give a bit more humanity to the principal character.

Although he was warned by his production staff about the potential hazard of filming at night with children and with explosives in the scene, Landis refused to change his production concept. He was also aware that California had strict rules about using children in filming, and these rules forbade youngsters working at night. The rules also require that a social-welfare worker be on the set to ensure that there are no risks to the children, and that person can actually stop the filming process if he or she feels there is some hazard. But even though it was suggested that they use dummies or midgets instead of children, Landis refused.

The actor chosen for the role of bigot Bill Connor was Vic Morrow. Morrow had played the part of a juvenile delinquent in the film *The Blackboard Jungle* in 1955, but more recently had been known primarily for his role in the television series *Combat*. He was happy to get a role in a big-budget film after several years of performing on the small screen.

Realizing they could not obtain two Asian children from the regular agents who represented child actors (since they were violating the law), the production team found two children informally and agreed to pay their parents $500 each for the filming. This was considerably more than the normal $90 paid for extra work. The children were six-year-old Renee Chen and seven-year-old My-Ca Dinh Le.

The Vietnam sequence was scheduled to be filmed at a place called Indian Dunes, off Highway 126, about an hour's drive west of Hollywood, on July 21, 1982. It would involve explosions, machine-gun fire, and, hovering above the actors, a helicopter with a powerful searchlight illuminating the figures below. Morrow, holding the children, would wade across a shallow stream as the explosives were detonated all around him.

Preparations and setup for the sequence took longer than expected, and the crew soon realized that there would not be enough time to do the scene, though they did shoot another sequence with the children in a hut when Connor first encounters them. Landis apologized for the delay and offered the parents an additional $500 for another night of filming. The parents agreed to have the kids (now very tired) return to participate again the following night.

The next day the children, each with a parent along, were picked up and brought back to the Indian Dunes location, where they waited in a trailer for their scene to be filmed. They were some distance from where the filming was occurring and were not aware that a previous sequence with Morrow had just been shot and the explosions had risen so high that they almost burned the actors and crewmen in the helicopter above. Helicopter pilot Dorcey Wingo was furious, as he was not told of the force of the explosions.

The next scene to be filmed would involve Morrow and the children. At 2:15 a.m., with six cameras ready to roll, Morrow took his position holding the two children and standing in the water. As the helicopter moved into position overhead, thirty-five feet above the water, director Landis shouted into his radio, "Lower! Lower! Lower!" Wingo, the pilot, was surprised, but lowered the craft to twenty-four feet.

Landis gave the signal for Morrow to move with the children, and then signaled the explosions to begin around them. The fourth and fifth explosion sent a fireball into the air that engulfed the tail of the helicopter. Its tail rotor damaged, the aircraft began to spin out of control. All around, the explosions had created fires and the crew scrambled for safety. In the helicopter, pilot Dorcey Wingo desperately tried to control the spinning craft, but he could not. The helicopter descended, landing upright in the water, then turned on its side. Morrow had lost his grip on Renee Chen, and part of the helicopter came down on her, crushing her to death. The still-spinning rotor blades cut through the water, decapitating Vic Morrow and My-Ca Dinh Le.

After an investigation, five men were put on trial as responsible parties in the deaths that occurred at Indian Dunes: director John Landis, helicopter pilot Dorcey Wingo, associate producer George Folsey Jr., unit production manager Dan Allingham, and special-effects foreman Paul Stewart. The charge was involuntary manslaughter. Interestingly, the prosecution did not charge Landis and his staff with violation of the child labor laws—a charge that could have easily been proven (though it was only a misdemeanor).

The trial began on August 28, 1986, and concluded nine months later, on May 29, 1987. The verdict? All five of the defendants were judged not guilty. The jurors felt that the prosecution had not proven that there was deliberate negligence on the set. The defense had pressed the issue that what happened that night was an unfortunate accident, and the jury, though skeptical, had accepted the testimony that validated this.

After the trial, John Landis would go on to direct the highly touted music video "Thriller" for Michael Jackson, in addition to several comedies that included *Spies Like Us* and *Coming to America* and some television documentaries.

As a result of the accident on the set of *The Twilight Zone,* there have been changes made to California's child labor laws and stricter enforcement of existing laws. There has, however, also been some relaxation of restrictions on children working at night, and it is very likely that some may still be working on sets without adherence to the state's child labor laws.

The parents of the two children who died sued the production company, and each collected $2 million in an out-of-court settlement. The daughters of Vic Morrow, Carrie Morrow and actress Jennifer Jason Leigh, also sued and settled out of court for an undisclosed amount.

The Twilight Zone accident may well have gotten more publicity than any other fatal occurrence on a movie set, but, unfortunately, it was hardly the first and would not be the last time a performer or crew member died as a result of filming a motion picture.

HOLLYWOOD FACTS AND TRIVIA

- The first movie filmed in Hollywood was D. W. Griffith's *In Old California,* made in 1910. It was a ten-minute melodrama set in California in the 1800s, when the area was Mexican territory.

- The first movie studio in Hollywood was the Nestor Studio, which opened in October 1911.

- The first feature film made in Hollywood was 1914's *The Squaw Man,* directed by Cecil B. DeMille and Oscar Apfel. DeMille filmed *The Squaw Man* three different times: in 1914, 1918, and 1931.

- The first film to be shown at the White House was D. W. Griffith's *The Birth of a Nation,* in 1915, for President Woodrow Wilson.

- The huge wall of Babylon set that D. W. Griffith had built for the film *Intolerance* stood at the corner of Hollywood and Sunset Boulevards for four years. It was eventually declared a fire hazard and was torn down in 1919. The new Highland Center at Hollywood Boulevard and Highland Avenue has an archway that is similar in size and decor to Griffith's set and was built as homage to the great director.

- For authenticity in filming sequences at the end of the modern story in *Intolerance,* D. W. Griffith used the services of Martin Aguerre, a former warden of Sing Sing Prison. Aguerre supervised the building of a gallows for the execution scene.

- Charlie Chaplin was the first actor to appear on the cover of *Time* magazine, on July 6, 1925. He was knighted in March 1975 at Buckingham Palace, just three miles from the slums where he grew up.

- Actress Mabel Normand was once a professional model and posed for such famous artists as Charles Dana and James Montgomery Flagg.

- The first person to leave prints in the cement in front of Grauman's Chinese Theater was actress Norma Talmadge, who accidentally stepped into newly laid cement in 1926. From this misstep, a tradition was started.

- *Wings* was the first film to win an Academy Award for Best Picture, in 1927. It was also the only silent film to win the Oscar, since sound films began to be shown the following year.

- Although *The Jazz Singer* (1927) was the first feature film to use spoken dialogue (with two short dialogue scenes totaling just 354 words), *Don Juan* (1926) was the first feature with a sound track. The sound, however, was only a music score, performed by the 107-piece Philharmonic Orchestra, directed by Herman Heller.

- *King Kong* (1933) was originally slated to be titled *The Beast,* then *The Eighth Wonder of the World.*

- Among the actresses considered for the lead in *King Kong* were Jean Harlow and Ginger Rogers, a role that eventually went to Fay Wray.

- The giant ape is never called "King Kong" in the film, just "Kong." The exception is on the theater marquee toward the end, but this was added after most of the film was shot.

- Two of the eighteen-inch models of Kong had to have their skins removed each day of filming so that the bolts and screws could be retightened.

- The New York appearance of the ape in *King Kong* was originally to take place in Yankee Stadium, but the location was changed to a theater.

- *King Kong* was the only movie to open simultaneously at both New York's Roxy Theater and Radio City Music Hall, just a few blocks away.

- In the 1930s Lloyd's of London insured the life of popular child star Shirley Temple, but the policy stated the company would not pay if she met death or injury while drunk. At the time, she was seven years old.

- Among the rejected names for dwarfs in Disney's *Snow White and the Seven Dwarfs* (1937) were Jumpy, Hotsy, Shifty, Dirty, and Awful.

- At the 1937 Academy Awards, *Snow White and the Seven Dwarfs* received a special award: one full-size Oscar and seven small ones.

- The huge gates that had been used in *King Kong,* along with other old sets on the back lot of RKO Studios, were set on fire as part of the "burning of Atlanta" scene in *Gone With the Wind.*

- Because of the Motion Picture Code, Rhett Butler's line "Frankly, my dear, I don't give a damn" was also filmed as "Frankly, my dear, I don't care." Fortunately, the first choice was eventually the one used.

- At the premiere of *Gone With the Wind* in Atlanta in 1939, black cast members were not permitted to attend due to Georgia's racial segregation laws.

- In addition to being the first film in which Orson Welles appeared, *Citizen Kane* also marked the film debuts of Joseph Cotten, Agnes Moorhead, and Ruth Warrick.

- One of the most often quoted movie lines is "Play it again, Sam," but this line is never actually spoken in *Casablanca* (1942). In the film Humphrey Bogart says, "Play it!" and Ingrid Bergman says, "Play it, Sam. Play 'As Time Goes By.'"

- The first commercial television station west of the Mississippi River was KTLA, which began broadcasting in January 1947.

- Walt Disney received four Academy Awards—during just one ceremony (1953). He won for Best Cartoon, Best Feature Documentary, Best Short Documentary, and Best Short Subject. In all, Disney holds the record for winning the most Academy Awards (twenty-six) and also the most nominations (sixty-four).

- The Hollywood Walk of Fame was created and the first star placed in 1958.

- Ub Iwerks, who worked for Walt Disney and who many believe was the real creator of Mickey Mouse, did the special effects for the 1963 Alfred Hitchcock film *The Birds*.

- Marilyn Monroe was the first centerfold for *Playboy* magazine, in December 1953. This was the only issue in which the centerfold was called "Sweetheart of the Month."

- Though the Academy Awards were first presented in 1927, the first native Californian to win Best Actor was Gregory Peck for the film *To Kill a Mockingbird*—thirty-five years later, in 1962.

- Probably the shortest speech ever made at an Academy Awards ceremony was by Alfred Hitchcock when he received the Irving Thalberg Memorial Award in 1967 for his long career. The director said "Thank you" and left the stage.

- As of the 2000 census, the area of Los Angeles called Hollywood had a population of 210,777.

- In 2002 a campaign was initiated to have Hollywood secede from Los Angeles and become a separate, incorporated municipality. The referendum was put on the ballot but failed by a wide margin.

- Hollywood does not have its own government (since it is part of Los Angeles), but it does have an "Honorary Mayor." This job was held for many years by TV personality Johnny Grant, until his death in 2008.

- As of 2009 the film that has grossed more money than any other is *Titanic* (1997), with more than $1 billion earned internationally.

- As of 2009 only one family has produced three generations of Academy Award winners, the Hustons: Walter, for Best Supporting Actor in *The Treasure of the Sierra Madre* (1948); son John, Best Director for the same film; and John's daughter Anjelica, Best Supporting Actress for *Prizzi's Honor* in 1985.

BIBLIOGRAPHY

Aitken, Roy E. *The Birth of a Nation Story.* Middleburg, VA: William W. Denlinger, 1965.

Behlmer, Rudy. *America's Favorite Movies: Behind the Scenes.* New York: Frederick Ungar Publishing Company, 1982.

Berg, A. Scott. *Goldwyn: A Biography.* New York: Alfred A. Knopf, 1989.

Biskind, Peter. *Easy Riders, Raging Bulls.* New York: Simon and Schuster, 1998.

Bluestone, George. *Novels into Film.* Berkeley and Los Angeles: University of California Press, 1973.

Brown, Karl. *Adventures with D. W. Griffith.* New York: Farrar, Strauss and Giroux, 1973.

Brown, Peter Harry, and Patte B. Barham. *Marilyn: The Last Take.* New York: Penguin Books, 1992.

Brownlow, Kevin, and John Kobal. *Hollywood: The Pioneers.* New York: Alfred A. Knopf, 1979.

Capra, Frank. *The Name Above the Title: An Autobiography.* New York: Macmillan Company, 1971.

Chaplin, Charles. *My Autobiography.* New York: Simon and Schuster, 1964.

Christopher, Milbourne. *Houdini: The Untold Story.* New York: Thomas Y. Crowell Company, 1969.

Clarens, Carlos. *An Illustrated History of the Horror Film.* New York: Capricorn Books, 1968.

Cowie, Peter. *The Cinema of Orson Welles.* New York: A. S. Barnes and Co., 1965.

Eliot, Marc. *Walt Disney: Hollywood's Dark Prince.* New York: Carol Publishing Group, 1993.

Ellenberger, Allan. *Ramon Novarro.* Jefferson, North Carolina: McFarland, 1999.

Farber, Stephen, and Marc Green. *Outrageous Conduct: Art, Ego, and the Twilight Zone Case.* New York: William Morrow and Company, 1988.

Finch, Christopher. *The Art of Walt Disney.* New York: Harry N. Abrams, 1999.

Flamini, Roland. *Scarlett, Rhett, and a Cast of Thousands.* New York: MacMillan Publishing Co., 1975.

Fonda, Henry. *My Life.* With Howard Teichmann. New York: New American Library, 1981.

Fonda, Peter. *Don't Tell Dad.* New York: Hyperion, 1998.

Fowler, Gene. *Father Goose.* New York: Avon Books, 1974.

Fussell, Betty. *Mabel: Hollywood's First I-Don't-Care Girl.* New Haven and New York: Ticknor and Fields, 1982.

Gardner, Gerald. *The Censorship Papers.* New York: Dodd, Mead, and Company, 1987.

Goldner, Orville, and George E. Turner. *The Making of King Kong.* New York: Ballantine Books, 1975.

Griffith, D. W. *The Man Who Invented Hollywood: The Autobiography of D. W. Griffith.* Edited by James Hart. Louisville, KY: Touchstone Publishing Company, 1972.

Griffith, Mrs. D. W. *When the Movies Were Young.* New York and London: Benjamin Blom, 1925. Reissued 1968.

Gussow, Mel. *Don't Say Yes Until I Finish Talking: A Biography of Darryl F. Zanuck.* Garden City, NY: Doubleday and Company, 1971.

Haver, Ronald. *David O. Selznick's Hollywood.* New York: Alfred A. Knopf, 1980.

Henderson, Robert M. *D. W. Griffith: The Years at Biograph.* New York: Farrar, Strauss and Giroux, 1970.

——— . *D. W. Griffith: His Life and Work.* New York: Oxford University Press, 1972.

Higham, Charles. *Howard Hughes, The Secret Life.* New York: Berkley Books, 1994.

Holden, Anthony. *Behind the Oscar: The Secret History of the Academy Awards.* New York: Simon and Schuster, 1993.

Kalush, William, and Larry Sloman. *The Secret Life of Houdini.* New York: Atria Books, 2006.

Kirkpatrick, Sidney D. *A Cast of Killers.* New York: E. P. Dutton, 1986.

Labrecque, Ron. *Special Effects. Disaster at Twilight Zone: The Tragedy and the Trial.* New York: Charles Scribner's Sons, 1988.

Lahue, Kalton C., and Terry Brewer. *Kops and Custards: The Legend of Keystone Films.* Norman, OK: University of Oklahoma Press, 1968.

Larsen, Milt. *Hollywood Illusion: Magic Castle.* Hollywood, CA: Brookledge Corporation, 2000.

Lasky, Jesse L., with Don Weldon. *I Blow My Own Horn.* Garden City, NY: Doubleday and Company, 1957.

Leaming, Barbara. *Orson Welles: A Biography.* New York: Viking Penguin, 1985.

Macgowan, Kenneth. *Behind the Screen.* New York: Delacorte Press, 1965.

Marx, Arthur. *Goldwyn: A Biography of the Man Behind the Myth.* New York: W. W. Norton Company, 1976.

McBride, Joseph. *Frank Capra: The Catastrophe of Success.* New York: Simon and Schuster, 1992.

Medved, Harry, and Michael Medved. *The Hollywood Hall of Shame.* New York: Perigee Books, 1984.

Michael, Paul. *The Academy Awards: A Pictorial History.* New York: Bonanza Books, 1964.

Norman, Barry. *The Story of Hollywood.* New York: New American Library, 1987.

O'Dell, Paul. *Griffith and the Rise of Hollywood.* New York: A. S. Barnes and Company, 1970.

Parish, James Robert. *The Hollywood Book of Death.* Chicago and New York: Contemporary Books, 2002.

Ramsaye, Terry. *A Million and One Nights: A History of the Motion Picture.* New York: Simon and Schuster, 1926.

Robinson, David. *Chaplin: His Life and Art.* New York: McGraw Hill Book Company, 1985.

Ronnie, Art. *Locklear: The Man Who Walked on Wings.* Cranbury, NJ: A. S. Barnes and Company, 1973.

Rovin, Jeff. *Movie Special Effects.* Cranbury, NJ: A. S. Barnes and Company, 1977.

Schickel, Richard. *The Disney Version.* New York: Simon and Schuster, 1968.

———. *D. W. Griffith: An American Life.* New York: Simon and Schuster, 1984.

Sennett, Mack. *King of Comedy*. With Cameron Shipp. New York: Pinnacle Books, 1975.

Shipman, David. *The Great Movie Stars: The Golden Years*. New York: Crown Publishers, 1970.

Silverman, Kenneth. *Houdini!!!* New York: HarperCollins Publishers, 1996.

Slatzer, Robert F. *The Curious Death of Marilyn Monroe*. New York: Pinnacle Books, 1974.

Soares, Andre. *Beyond Paradise. The Life of Ramon Novarro*. New York: St. Martin's Press, 2002.

Sperling, Cass Warner, and Cork Millner, with Jack Warner Jr. *Hollywood Be Thy Name: The Warner Brothers Story*. Rocklin, CA: Prima Publishing, 1994.

Summers, Anthony. *Goddess: The Secret Lives of Marilyn Monroe*. New York: Macmillan Publishing Company, 1985.

Thomas, Bob. *Walt Disney: Magician of the Movies*. New York: Grosset and Dunlap, 1966.

Thomson, David. *Showman: The Life of David O. Selznick*. New York: Alfred A Knopf, 1992.

Walker, Alexander. *The Shattered Silents*. New York: William Morrow and Company, 1979.

INDEX

ABOUT THE AUTHOR

Gerald Schiller is the author of nine books and more than a hundred articles that have appeared in magazines and newspapers including the *Los Angeles Times, Film News, Mystery Readers Journal,* and *Aviation History*. A former teacher, he has also written and directed documentary and educational films. He regularly performs as a magician and is a performing member of the world-famous Hollywood Magic Castle. He and his wife, Esther, have two grown children and one grandchild, and live in Southern California. For more information about Gerald, please visit his Web site www.geraldaschiller.com.